Additional Praise for *Betting on You*

"Irreverent, funny, direct. As a former HR professional, Ruettimann offers transparency about jobs in America that readers will find very appealing." **—Booklist**

"Why are some people successful at work while others are stuck? If you've ever wondered why you're not getting ahead, Laurie Ruettimann's answer might surprise you: it's probably you. *Betting on You* is a powerful reminder that the most successful leaders run their lives like businesses, prioritize their professional development, and believe their own hype."

—Cy Wakeman, *New York Times* bestselling author of *The Reality-Based Rules of the Workplace* and *No Ego*

"Never before have we been so collectively burnt out. But with pragmatic advice and an infectious jumpstart attitude, Laurie Ruettimann provides the groundwork—and inspiration—needed to change course."

—Daniel H. Pink, #1 *New York Times* bestselling author of *When, Drive,* and *To Sell Is Human*

BETTING ON YOU

BETTING ON YOU

HOW TO PUT YOURSELF FIRST

AND (FINALLY)

TAKE CONTROL OF YOUR CAREER

Laurie Ruettimann

A Holt Paperback
Henry Holt and Company
New York

Holt Paperbacks
Henry Holt and Company
Publishers since 1866
120 Broadway
New York, New York 10271
www.henryholt.com

A Holt Paperback® and 🅗® are registered trademarks of
Macmillan Publishing Group, LLC.

Distributed in Canada by Raincoast Book Distribution Limited

The Library of Congress has cataloged the hardcover edition as follows:

Names: Ruettimann, Laurie, author.
Title: Betting on you : how to put yourself first and (finally) take
   control of your career / Laurie Ruettimann.
Description: First edition. | New York : Henry Holt and Company,
   2021. | Includes index.
Identifiers: LCCN 2020020192 (print) | LCCN 2020020193 (ebook) |
   ISBN 9781250269805 (hardcover) | ISBN 9781250289799 (ebook)
Subjects: LCSH: Career development. | Success—Psychological aspects.
Classification: LCC HF5381 .R78554 2021 (print) | LCC HF5381
   (ebook) | DDC 650.1—dc23
LC record available at https://lccn.loc.gov/2020020192
LC ebook record available at https://lccn.loc.gov/2020020193

ISBN: 9781250838377 (trade paperback)

Our books may be purchased in bulk for promotional, educational, or
business use. Please contact your local bookseller or the Macmillan Corporate
and Premium Sales Department at (800) 221-7945, extension 5442, or by
e-mail at MacmillanSpecialMarkets@macmillan.com.

Originally published in hardcover in 2021 by Henry Holt and Company

First Holt Paperbacks Edition 2022

Designed by Meryl Sussman Levavi

Printed in the United States of America

3   5   7   9   10   8   6   4   2

For Sawyer and Lucas—
I'm betting on you.

nobody can save you but yourself and you're worth saving. it's a war not easily won but if anything is worth winning then this is it.

—CHARLES BUKOWSKI

Contents

BETTING ON YOU

Introduction:
Surprise, Work Is Broken

Y ou are not human if you haven't, sometimes, hated your job.

I worked in human resources for Pfizer, a major pharmaceutical company. It makes three drugs almost all Americans take at one time or another: Lipitor for your heart, Viagra for your other heart, and Xanax for just about everything else. Before I started at Pfizer, my career in HR was on fire—if you can be on fire in the sedate world of human resources. I pursued just about every credential and was certified to teach executive leadership courses, communication skills, and advanced methods of sourcing and recruiting.

But once I got the job at Pfizer, things changed. Often I felt my biggest accomplishment was just making it through the day. Within weeks, I knew it was a bad fit. The job I had been promised on paper—one with strategic challenges, big goals, and a lot of autonomy—turned out to be a crummy position surrounded by narrow-minded people with petty grievances and a fear of upsetting the chain of command. Probably a lot like yours.

At most companies, the culture may be messy or borderline toxic. Often, conflict isn't addressed, communication sucks or consists of an endless stream of Slack messages, and nobody ever responds to emails. Actually, sometimes they do—but only to the first question and not the other four, or they all respond at once, late in the day, right when you clock out and want to cook dinner.

Perhaps your office is ultrapolitical. The senior-level leaders all went to the same university or attend church together. Everybody on the leadership team carries the same handbag or wears the same brand of shoes. Your coworker invited your boss to his wedding, and now, in a strange coincidence, that person keeps getting all the best assignments.

Or maybe your office is okay, the people are fine, but there's a nagging voice in your head that keeps asking, "Is this as good as it gets?" Well, I am here to tell you that your career, and your life, can get a hell of a lot better—even if you are someone like me, who loves working but *hates* the workplace.

You picked up this book because you need help—regardless of your education, your background, or your chosen industry. I have a corporate background, and the examples in this book are pulled from my experience, but all work in the twenty-first century has the potential to be demoralizing—white- and blue-collar alike.

After all, what's the difference between someone who has a job in a factory and someone who writes code when your boss is a jerk, your career has stalled, and your paycheck doesn't cover your bills? I'm going to show you how to prioritize your physical, emotional, and financial well-being so you'll be a better colleague, supervisor, parent, partner, and friend.

The world of work has changed since I started writing this book. My initial goal was to critique leaders and HR departments without being too cynical. My challenge was to be candid but offer a ray of hope. Now, I have to restrain myself from saying, "I told you so."

We live in an era of uncertainty, but we are lying to ourselves if we believe that systems, processes, and programs were ever designed to make workers feel secure. From the dot-com bubble to the Great Recession, work has been restructured by consultants and leadership teams so that people in power will always end up doing just fine. It's employees, and particularly those in the BIPOC community, who shoulder the disproportionate amount of risk.

In that way, pandemics, civil unrest, and financial meltdowns make the book's tenets all the more applicable. This book will help you create your own culture within your company, one that values you as a person ahead of being a worker. You'll get advice and guidance to help you form better relationships and guard against unfair labor practices, both individually and systemically. In short, I'm here to teach you how to be your own HR department—a skill that's needed so you can advocate for yourself and good work, anticipate bad news, and plan for your future on your own terms.

Maybe you dream of taking a risk, becoming an entrepreneur, and doing your own thing—but you're afraid of financial ruin. Perhaps you have a partner and kids or other family members who depend on you for a paycheck. Let's start planning the next phase of your life now, whether you're in your current position or navigating the world of unemployment and redundancy. Because if you want to improve your career—and your life—it's time to plan for a better future and bet on *yourself* first.

Betting on You is a twenty-first-century employee handbook that teaches you how to prioritize your well-being, take thoughtful risks with your career, build community, become a person who is always learning and being challenged—and be your own agent of change in the process. In short, I will use my years of HR experience to show you exactly what you need to do to make your current situation not just tolerable but remarkably better. And I'll also show you how to blow it all up and start fresh.

Along the way, you will read stories about actual people who have actual jobs, illustrating how to put your house in order, clean up your life, and organize your health and money so you have real alternatives. Some of these stories are embarrassing and ridiculous. They reflect the totally absurd world of modern life. Rest assured that some names and time lines have been changed, identifying details have been altered and, in a few cases, combined to protect the innocent and to get to the point: it's time to put yourself first and finally take control of your career.

When you're done with this book, you will feel empowered to demand more from your life and workplace, and you will know how you can act as your own one-person HR department to change things—even if the folks in the real HR department do nothing and the world seems hard to predict.

And if none of that works, this book will help you leave your current role and find someplace better.

I know it all firsthand because I took my own medicine and evolved my dead-end job into a career that improves people's lives. And I've done it without totally compromising my values. If there's anything I've learned along the way, it's this: you fix your world by fixing yourself first.

1

Find Your Tijuana

WELL-BEING AND BEING
IN THE WORKPLACE

> If you don't understand yourself you don't
> understand anybody else.
>
> —Nikki Giovanni

Back when Bill Clinton was president and everybody was wearing "The Rachel" haircut, I was a first-generation college student with no financial or emotional support from my working-class family. During the day, I attended classes that I couldn't afford at an overpriced liberal arts university. In the evening, I was part of the gig economy before it was cool. My primary job was to answer phones in the university's Religious Studies Department to fulfill my work-study obligations. But I also spent time as an usher at a theater, a babysitter, and a clerk at Blockbuster

Video, where I collected fees from customers who forgot to rewind their VHS tapes.

None of those jobs paid very well. My multiple paychecks added up to about $100/week, which was just enough money to cover rent and food for myself and my cat, named Lucy. During my junior year, my landline was shut off. Lucy had an expensive vet bill, and I had to make a choice between textbooks and the utilities. Soon after, I got into a car accident and couldn't afford the repairs, so I took matters into my own hands and used a bungee cord to attach the bumper to the frame.

Instead of focusing on the positive things about being in college—the opportunity to learn and grow or the benefit of having newfound friends with different points of view—I felt like a middle-aged man in the suburbs saddled with a wife, two kids, and chronic debt.

At one point, I thought about dropping out of school altogether to catch up on my bills. I sought the advice of an academic adviser, who told me that taking time off would be a disaster. Leaving college, even for a semester, would ruin my chances at upward mobility. She encouraged me to bet on my future and take out yet another unsubsidized student loan from Sallie Mae with an 8.25 percent interest rate.

While it's true that a college degree once helped a generation of people leapfrog into the middle class, my adviser was biased toward the institution that paid her bills. Instead of helping me sort through my financial and academic challenges, she retroactively assigned positive qualities to my education rather than make me think critically about my future. And despite the warning signs that my student loan debt would be impossible to pay off and might bankrupt my future, she told me not to walk away from school because of the time and energy I'd already invested.*

I chose to stay in school, but I was sick of living below the poverty level. I asked myself, "What would a rich person do?"

First and foremost, rich people have substantial income.

I went back to my university and asked for help. Someone poked around and found a paid internship that didn't require a business background. It was at a candy factory next to a minimum-security prison. When I asked for a description of the job, they didn't have a lot of details.

"You're in a department called HR. Good luck, kid."

Let me say right away that I never meant to work in human resources. In fact, I didn't even know what "HR" meant when I went to the interview. The hiring manager explained that HR enforced company policies, made sure everybody was paid on time, and created systems to prevent employee lawsuits. None of that made sense to me, but I perked up when I learned that the job paid $8/hour and all the licorice and gummy candy I could eat.

_____

* This is called the "sunk-cost fallacy," where you continue to spend money because you've already spent it and you don't want that previous investment to feel like it was a waste of time.

I hated licorice, especially old-timey black licorice that tastes like a spicy roof shingle, but minimum wage in America was only $4.25 an hour back then. This new job nearly doubled my income. The HR director said, "You'll have a career path and lots of opportunities. Maybe one day you can contribute to a retirement plan."

Those early days were rough. I kept my full-time course load but worked twenty-five hours each week filing paperwork and guarding the company fax machine against improper use or abuse. (Even back then, companies didn't trust people with technology.)

Right away, there were signs that I wasn't a good cultural fit for the job. My head was shaved, and I had piercings above my eyebrows. I didn't own professional clothes. After a week on the job, my boss took me aside and told me that she believed in my potential but asked me to clean up my appearance. She wanted me to grow out my hair, find something conservative to wear, and take out my piercings. I went to JCPenney and bought a few pairs of sensible black pants and cardigan sweaters. I also traded in my generic combat boots for penny loafers from Payless ShoeSource. Then I asked a friend with pliers to meet me in the candy factory parking lot and help me cut through the crusty metal jewelry in my face.

Once my appearance was less of an issue, people could see that I had talent. I didn't bristle at faxing memos or making copies. I made friends with the hourly employees and listened to their stories, which meant that I always had the inside scoop on gossip and factory intrigue. And I was an excellent recruiter, able to read a résumé and understand instinctively if someone was a good fit for a job.

Who knew these skills were within me?

After graduation, I dreamed of attending graduate school but was afraid of taking on more debt. I grew my hair into a bob with very unflattering bangs and found a new job at a company called Monsanto, where I earned $16/hour as a contract recruiter. I hired engineers and chemists. I still wasn't allowed to be punk rock, but I was grateful for the paycheck. My phone was no longer disconnected, my rent was paid, and I could afford groceries and vet visits for Lucy.

But it's not like this job made me rich. I was just getting by now, albeit resentfully. There were mornings when I drove my jacked-up Honda past a line of protesters who objected to Monsanto's product called Posilac—a hormone given to cows to increase their production of milk—and another product called Roundup, which is a controversial weed killer. I sympathized with their beliefs but wondered how these men and women had the freedom to take time off.

About two months into the job, a man walked into my office. He was tall, handsome, and a little older than I was. He introduced himself as Ken, and my world was never the same. He was a chemical engineer who made drugs for Monsanto and needed help hiring for his team. I don't remember what exactly we talked about, but I remember how he made me feel—comfortable, beautiful with my bobbed hair and cardigans, and seen.

We dated on and off for a few years before we married.

Eventually, I ditched Monsanto and moved on to the next HR job, which paid more. Ken enjoyed his job, was promoted several times, and we were relocated in 2004 when Pfizer and Monsanto merged. That's when Pfizer offered me the opportunity to interview for a role in the HR department. Was I interested? Would I think about it?

I wasn't excited about working for the world's largest drug company, but they described a role that would coach and advise leaders on strategic HR initiatives and change management strategies across the enterprise. They talked about infinite opportunities to learn from some of the best business leaders in the world. And they promised a culture of inclusion, collaboration, and transparency. It still felt like I was selling out to a behemoth drug company, but I thought I could learn and, to be honest, it paid more than any other job in the area.

What I didn't know is that Pfizer faced what many other organizations faced at various points: too many corporate employees and not enough drugs in the pipeline. There were layoffs, and the company needed someone who could get up in the air and make it happen. That was me.

Nobody was honest about the job duties when I flew to New York City and met with the HR team. Instead, a VP in human resources talked at length about himself and warned me, "We believe in chain of command around here. You can make all the mistakes you want. But if you make a mistake and don't tell me, I'll rip your head off and shit down your throat."

I thought he was joking. He sounded like Dr. Evil from the Austin Powers movies, but the dude was serious and, also, super impressed with himself for sounding so badass. Then he looked me in the eye and asked, "What's it going to take to get you to accept an offer?"

"Money," I said. "Lots of money."

And sure enough, they gave it to me. My role at Pfizer paid a healthy base salary with a bonus and stock options, plus all the trimmings of a corporate job—excellent health care, a retirement plan, stock options, paid time off, mobile phone reimbursement, and lots of wellness perks. It's hard to turn down a lucrative compensation package, especially when you're saddled with student loan debt, but the rip-your-head-off speech was a clear sign that this money would be hard-earned.

To prepare myself, I read a few self-help books from the local library. I learned how to do deep-breathing exercises. On the night before my first day, I hung a sign over my bathroom mirror that said, NO ONE CAN MAKE YOU FEEL INFERIOR WITHOUT YOUR CONSENT.

Ken asked, "Isn't that overkill?"

I said, "You haven't met Dick."

My instincts were right. The emerging leadership role that was promised? It was a joke. And the promise of a collaborative and supportive environment was garbage, too. It didn't take long to discover that the job at Pfizer was less glamorous than promised. Instead of being involved in strategic HR decisions across the enterprise—or even having an opportunity to be mentored by the people who made those decisions—I flew to places like Terre Haute, Indiana, and Lincoln, Nebraska, to inform people their jobs were over.

When I tried to talk to colleagues about my broken job, I faced the same issues as back during my college internship, when I couldn't find anybody who looked or acted like me. I worked with middle-aged IT dudes and uptight older women in Manhattan who sported French manicures and fancy scarves. They had different lives, backgrounds, and interests. And everybody continued to use acronyms and buzzwords to communicate.

For example, the company wasn't firing people with hearts and souls. Instead, it was capitalizing on corporate synergies and eliminating institutional inefficiencies by creating COEs (centers of excellence) to better serve our stakeholders. It was also reducing bloat and reinvesting in organizational transformation to produce greater, long-term shareholder value.

Pick your phrase: none of it made any sense.

While the layoffs were happening, Pfizer hired a new chief HR officer and added yet another layer of bureaucracy over my VP of HR.* This new HR leader used the

* https://fortune.com/2011/07/28/inside-pfizers-palace-coup/.

company helicopter to commute from her home in Maryland to our New York City headquarters every day. She wasn't the only executive with personal helicopter privileges, but the optics were awful. I struggled to do my job in an environment where executives fiddled while Rome burned.

What's worse is that I got caught up in the hype and developed a form of Stockholm syndrome where I volunteered for duties I didn't want and responsibilities that taxed my work–life balance, just to prove that I deserved more.

More what?

Who knows? More money, more responsibility, more recognition, more love, more self-esteem, more respect. More face time with executives who would never like me or appreciate my contributions. More visibility with leaders who looked down at people like me, who didn't live in the right part of the country or attend prestigious universities. And more opportunities to impress people who would never see value in my contributions.

The more I tried, the less I liked my job. And the more hours I spent working, the less I technically earned per hour. Suddenly that six-figure salary felt like I was back at Blockbuster Video—except the people at the video store smiled more and said hello.

Why was HR so terrible? When you're in human resources, you see the underbelly of the entire organization. Much of your time is spent refereeing fights between grown-ass adults and holding people accountable for doing the bare minimum—and that's just in HR itself. Then there's the crazy stuff.

Have you ever had a coworker dress up like a baby and wear nothing but a bonnet and diaper on Halloween? Have you ever heard of someone who called in sick for work because their dog died, only to have that same dog die again two months later? Has anyone ever asked you for advice on how to drink at a company party, "accidentally" fall, and file a worker's compensation claim?

Every day was a journey into the mystery of deviant human behavior. I wondered why people were such jerks. I couldn't figure out why they repeatedly made the same mistakes. It was a mystery as to why adults couldn't solve their own basic problems around conflict and communication. Whenever the phone would ring with an employee-relations issue, I'd shake my head and wonder when the robots would finally take over. Some days, it felt like automation and artificial intelligence couldn't come soon enough.

But instead of pursuing an MBA or taking additional management courses to develop my ideas on the future of work, I felt angry and stuck. When I was at my best, I was indifferent and uncaring. At my worst, I was an obnoxious asshole.

But my colleagues were terrible, too.

I had five bosses in three years who took one look at the dysfunctional landscape of our HR department and found different opportunities as fast as possible. The first was nice enough and treated me to dinners when I was in

New York City. Once, we ate at the Four Seasons restaurant in Midtown Manhattan. For weeks after, I told anybody who would listen about the restaurant's signature dessert of finely spun cotton candy. It doesn't take much to make a basic bitch like myself feel rich.

My second boss was a former sales leader who was transferred into human resources, and he forgot to invite me to the holiday party. When I asked him about it, he said, "Oh, yeah, sorry about that. You wouldn't have enjoyed it." (Actually, that's true. But it doesn't make it any less hurtful.)

The boss after him repeatedly called me Laura instead of Laurie, which didn't end until I called her Denise instead of Diana. And yet another boss gave me feedback on my attitude, saying not to be offended but, if it weren't for our common employer, we would not be friends.

I replied, "I'm not offended. We're not friends now."

And that was that. On the surface, things looked fine. I was staying afloat. But if you looked closer, you could see that I was getting closer and closer to drowning.

Then the day came when I had to tell Ken he was losing his job. Pfizer tried to develop a cholesterol drug that was better than Lipitor and failed.* The R&D department was reconfigured, and my husband's division was impacted. Nobody in HR was allowed to tell me the news before it was announced, but nobody in HR can keep a secret. I caught wind of the gossip and tried to warn

---

* https://www.wsj.com/articles/SB119733600536720234.

my husband over dinner, telling him that his entire team would be laid off at an upcoming meeting.

"What do you know? You work in HR."

Over a decade later, his comment still stings. But I also remember the look on Ken's face when he came home the following night and apologized for being so dismissive. I was right, and he had lost his job. The news rocked me hard when it finally happened—just like I was back in college trying to feed my cat and pay my bills.

Intellectually, I knew we would be fine. But until Ken found a new job, I couldn't quit. Someone had to provide health insurance, and that someone was me. I was officially stuck.

WHAT WOULD COURTNEY LOVE DO?

It's easy to tell people to quit a bad job and find a new one, but it rarely gets better.

Fifty-one percent of people are not engaged. Here's what that means: Put down this book. Make eye contact with someone. One of you dreads going to work. (And maybe it's you.) Meanwhile, 17 percent of workers are actively *disengaged*. That's one out of five employees who hate their jobs enough to steal food out of the refrigerator or sabotage whatever the rest of their teams are trying to accomplish. I hope that's not you.

Bob Sutton, a business professor at Stanford and author of *The No Asshole Rule*, once told me that the best thing you can do for yourself is to bet on the future and quit a toxic job. Yes, there are short-term coping mechanisms that alleviate some pain, but his research shows that the best thing you can do for your mental and physical well-being is to leave completely and never look back.

But what if you're stuck? Or what if you don't want to leave because you suspect that you're just temporarily frustrated and things might get better? While quitting is the right answer for some situations, it's not a satisfying or realistic path for most adults. And it wasn't an option for me at Pfizer. Not yet, anyway.

I spent a year at Pfizer killing time and waiting for change. When no cavalry rode into town to fix my life, I went on the Internet and looked for answers on how to reboot my career. Even back then, much of the Web was garbage, filled with inspirational quotes and articles about following your passions and dreams. Very few websites were dedicated to honest and pragmatic career advice. That's when I decided to try to answer my career questions by starting a blog about the behind-the-scenes world of HR.

That's right. I anonymously blogged while employed at Pfizer.

My traffic grew quickly because there weren't many blogs out there about human resources and the truth about how decisions are made in a corporate environment. Luckily for me, I could operate in the shadows. Few people understood what was happening online, and though once in a while someone at the office would ask about a new thing called "social media," I just played dumb and hoped nobody found my blog or social profiles.

Nobody did, or, if they knew, they didn't care.

Blogging wasn't a solution to all of my problems, but it was a solid start. Without even knowing it, I learned something new as a writer and social media marketer. I was building a new portfolio of professional skills while also pursuing an activity because it was interesting rather than just for the money.

But I felt lonely and isolated from spending too much time on the road by myself, laying off people all across Pfizer. Already out of shape when I joined Pfizer, my weight crept up with every new trip to fire people. I am five feet tall, and, at my heaviest, ballooned up to 159 pounds. My size began to impact my ability to get stuff done. I couldn't run across the airport to catch a connecting flight without losing my breath, and my body was perpetually sore.

Now, size is not indicative of health. Some people are technically overweight and do triathlons, lift weights, and run a nine-minute mile. Other people are skinny but don't have enough cardio endurance to walk up a flight of stairs. There are healthy-looking women with high cholesterol and larger men who look heavy but are in excellent health. Weight is only one data point for health. Mind-set is another.

My mind-set? Well, it was also in the dumps. Nothing made me happy. Not my marriage, my family, or even my cats. All I did was complain about life and consume sugar, fat, and salt to boost my mood. When people who loved me tried to coach me out of a state of learned helplessness, I lashed out and whined about being a victim while still cashing my paycheck.

I'm lucky I still have friends.

And most of all, my sleep suffered. It was hard to get out of bed, and early morning meetings at Pfizer were impossible. I would ask my husband to wake me before he left for work, but most of the time I'd roll back over and try to get more sleep. Sure, I had an alarm clock next to my bed, but it wasn't enough. I also had to set an alarm in another room. If I was in a hotel room on the road, I would set the alarm on my phone and on my bedside table but I also asked the concierge for a wake-up call. I told them, "Keep calling. If I don't answer, send someone up to knock on the door."

Once out of bed, I'd have some coffee and take medication. Sometimes we're depressed because of biology. Other times, it's the circumstances in our lives and the choices we make. In my case, it was all three. Pharmaceutical drugs can't fix career-induced depression, but I tried just about every drug on the market to be sure. Prozac. Zoloft. Wellbutrin. Paxil. Lexapro. BuSpar. Zyprexa. Risperdal. Seroquel. Remeron. Neurontin. Klonopin. Trazodone. Topamax. Cymbalta. Ativan. Xanax. Heavy drugs for someone my size, and none of them worked.

Even worse is that each drug came with a trial period to determine whether I could tolerate the side effects, the most common side effect being weight gain. My size changed so rapidly that one of my colleagues in IT asked if I was pregnant. (Those IT dudes have no filter.)

I realize it's hard to feel sorry for someone like me, who earned six figures and couldn't get out of bed in the morning, but there are real-world consequences for people who work in meaningless jobs that don't contribute emotionally to the world.

In his book *Bullshit Jobs: A Theory*, David Graeber writes about the existential problems facing corporate professionals whose jobs are pointless and exist only to support hegemonic corporations run amok. Many of those workers languish all day on the Internet—hanging out on Twitter and Facebook—trying to look busy.

I had one of those bullshit jobs. There was no purpose in my life other than implementing cost-cutting initiatives that didn't make a difference in the company's bottom line. And, even when I did my best, nobody liked me or thanked me for it.

During one of these trips across the country to fire people, I felt especially sad and lonely at a downtrodden and desolate airport in the middle of America. I grabbed a big bottle of Pepsi and a bag of Starburst candy for dinner. To take my mind off my problems, I bought a tabloid magazine from an airport bookstore. That's when I stumbled on an article that said Courtney Love got a lap band in Mexico.

Allegedly. She has denied it.*

---

* https://people.com/celebrity/courtney-love-denies-gastric-band-surgery/.

You might be like—Who's Courtney Love? How do I know that name?

I was like—What's a lap band?

Courtney Love is the gritty, punk rock ex-wife of Nirvana front man Kurt Cobain. That much, I knew. At that time in American history, she was in the news for her dramatic weight loss. But I knew nothing about weight-loss surgery or the emerging phenomenon of "medical tourism."

iPhones weren't around yet, and all I had was my heavy laptop with the nubby red ball in the center that was always dirty. The computer didn't even have Wi-Fi. I had to fly to my location and physically log on to the Internet to learn more about weight-loss surgery.

When I finally got online in my hotel room, it didn't take long to fall down a rabbit hole and read about medical tourism, weight-loss surgery, and dozens of celebrities who had discounted plastic surgery in Mexico.

Allegedly.

Thank goodness for Wikipedia and WebMD. I learned that a lap band is a medical device that wraps around your stomach and restricts the flow of food, causing you to lose weight slowly and steadily. Or so the marketing materials claim. At the time, it was only available to morbidly obese people and Hollywood stars who could cheat the system and pay for medical tourism in Tijuana, Brazil, or Singapore.

I was transfixed and thought, "Wow, money solves problems."

And I wasn't wrong. Money might not bring you happiness in a traditional sense, but it gives you options and helps you solve problems. In fact, corporations know that the single most effective way to solve a problem is to throw money at it. They deny it, but it's true. Need help to implement change in management initiatives? Hire a team of experts. Did you lose a high-profile CEO? Get another one. Can't solve a manufacturing challenge? Get a consultant. Need insights on what your competitors are doing? Pay for better data.

Pfizer fired people around the world but still spent cash to solve enterprise challenges. We spent money on renovating buildings to create open-office environments. We spent money on management consultants who helped us navigate organizational changes. And we spent money on large compensation packages to attract talented executives who would otherwise flee a toxic environment like ours.

When a company like Pfizer faces challenges, it reallocates the budget to maintain its dominance in the marketplace. Leaders don't have anxiety issues about collecting their paychecks or investing in their pet projects. They don't wonder if a competitor like Novartis deserves more success this quarter. Businesses weigh the short-term costs against the long-term benefits of investing in themselves, and they spend money to make money.

Do you realize what that means?

Companies put themselves first.

If I wanted to fix work, and my attitude toward it, I

had to be like Pfizer and play a bigger, better game. I had to consider my long-term interests, invest in my future, and put myself first.

The first thing I questioned was the story I told myself. Was I really stuck in this job? What benefits did I gain from continued employment? Could I make some short-term sacrifices and improve my long-term options? Was a career in the trenches of HR worth the physical and emotional toll on my body? What did I dream of doing with my life, and what could I do in six months to change?

Sitting in that hotel room in the heartland of America, a bigger vision of my life emerged. With a little money allocated to the proper expenditures, I could be anything I wanted to be: rock star, runner, amateur athlete, business leader, or maybe even a real writer who publishes something more substantial than her blog.

My bullshit job at Pfizer didn't have to be anything more than a blip on my résumé, but it would take an external intervention of epic proportions to change my life and officially end my career at the world's largest global pharmaceutical company.

That's when I decided to get a lap band in Mexico.

TIJUANA DREAMING ON A WINTER'S DAY

What's the craziest thing your partner or spouse has ever told you?

My husband heard my plan to get a lap band in Mexico and was like, *No, that's not happening. That's insane.*

He wasn't wrong. Getting a lap band because I read about it on the Internet seemed insane. Couldn't I find another way to put myself first?

"You're attractive and lovely without medical intervention," Ken said. "But, if you want to lose weight, have more self-control. Wouldn't hurt to cut your calories. If there's one thing you could do tomorrow, it's get more exercise."

These are the pragmatic and unhelpful things that thin people say about well-being.

But then Ken also said, "Other than depression, you have your health. Why would you do something so risky?"

That's when I stopped him and argued that if you're sad and dejected about your job or life's circumstances, then you don't have your health. And I was ready to change that.

I channeled my inner badass and contacted a weight-loss clinic in Tijuana. Remember, it's the early part of the twenty-first century with no Angie's List or Google Reviews to check this place out. We didn't have recommendation engines like Yelp or OpenTable. Even a long-distance call was expensive.

When I phoned the clinic in Mexico, they connected me to an English-speaking receptionist who explained that a lap band is a straightforward procedure. Not quite outpatient, but not a lengthy ordeal. The surgeon would poke a few holes in my abdomen, wrap a band around my stomach to slow down the flow of food and make me feel full, and then glue me up with stitches.

Yeah, sounds easy.

I asked about having the lap band monitored and adjusted. What if it was too loose or too tight? What if it felt uncomfortable? Would my insurance cover my follow-up visits back in America?

The receptionist told me that any bariatric doctor or surgeon in the United States could easily access my lap band and make adjustments in an office by sticking a needle full of saline into my belly. Did I have questions?

The woman grew impatient as I continued to inquire about the procedure, clearly eager to close the deal. She pushed for a down payment for the procedure. Did I want to reboot my life with a fresh start and better health outcomes? Don't I believe in wellness?

She didn't have to ask twice. I wired her $4,000 via PayPal and took a deep breath.

Several weeks later, I paid off the remaining balance—another $4,000 via PayPal—and got ready to travel to San Diego. Yes, my lap band was only $8,000 cash. Crazy-cheap compared to the American health system where the cost of the surgery was approximately three times that amount, but still a lot of money for the average Mexican citizen who might not have access to the health care and services offered at those border-town clinics.

While packing for Tijuana, I read a long series of forum posts for people who had plastic surgery in Mexico and other parts of Central America. Privileged white people can be racist, but there were serious issues happening in Mexico at the time. Back then, drug cartel kidnappings were on the rise, and the US Department of State flat-out warned people not to go. An average of six American citizens were kidnapped each month.*

The online hysteria didn't match what I knew about Tijuana. Having visited there several times as a child, I knew it to be a vibrant and welcoming place. I have warm memories of taking the monorail from San Diego to the Mexican border, and I can recall playing with local children and running through the stalls at the open-air markets as my family ate lunch.

But in the years since I had been to Mexico, the political and social landscape changed dramatically because of US foreign policy and the so-called war on drugs. If I had to go, the advice online was to carry $1,000 in cash for bribes, broken down into ten 100-dollar bills in separate envelopes. People online also advised me to tip anybody who might intervene with a kidnapping, although I'm not sure who might risk his life for a hundred bucks if I was snatched from the streets.

But, just in case, I went to the ATM and withdrew the funds.

---

* https://www.newsweek.com/kidnapped-mexico-border-93483.

Several weeks later, I flew into San Diego and hopped on a chartered van to Tijuana. The first stop was the hotel with other American guests who seemed to be in town for medical tourism, too. The lobby was full of men and women in large sunglasses, wearing gauze on their faces, or donning compression garments and walking slowly. I followed the advice online and gave the concierge a hundred bucks and asked him to keep me out of trouble. He nodded, like, *Okay, I don't know you, but I'll happily take this envelope full of cash.*

When I asked where I could get a quick bite to eat, he directed me to a local mall down the road. And by mall, he meant a promenade of repair shops, pharmacies, dentists' offices, and medical centers that were mostly empty and shuttered.

Today, the central zone of Tijuana is an emerging center of technology and innovation. It is flanked by retail hot spots such as Costco and McDonald's. But back in the day, it was much different. The main strip was known for meeting the needs of Americans under the age of twenty-one who liked to drink and party on the weekends, but the cartels had scared many tourists away. Local businesses suffered, and the streets appeared to be abandoned.

As I left the hotel, it was like a sepia-toned spaghetti western outside. The sun was hot. There was a dry wind that blew dust into my eyes. Tumbleweeds and sagebrush rolled down the road. And it's not just that I was the only blond-haired American walking around on the streets; I was the only person on the street, period.

After returning from my excursion to the mall, my second stop was the weight-loss clinic. Decorated in late-'90s shades of pink and white, it was tough to tell if this place was a hospital or a call center. Maybe it was both. Someone handed me a clipboard, directed me to a waiting room, and, eventually, asked me to step on a scale that looked like it was made for livestock. A nurse came into the room soon after and sighed, telling me I wasn't heavy enough for a lap band. It turns out that 159 pounds was under the recommended weight for surgery. She was sorry, but I had to go home.

I gave her a hundred bucks. She didn't move. Then I gave her another hundred dollars. Just like that, I qualified for surgery. Amazing, sometimes, how money solves problems.

Later that night, I contemplated my fate. The only thing between a successful surgery and coming home in a body bag was a couple of envelopes of cash, the competency of an unknown doctor, and an admittedly poorly researched medical procedure in a foreign country.

Would this be as easy as promised? Was I a victim of an international crime syndicate poised to steal my kidneys? Was I about to appear in the latest *Saw* sequel?

Fortune favors the bold. I was ready.

The procedure happened the following day, and it was easy. Not like getting a facial, but also not as painful as I'd imagined. I had a personal nurse, my room was super-clean, and the surgeon had a kinder bedside manner than the American doctor who removed my tonsils. The day after the surgery, I had a massage and didn't need pain medicine—just anti-inflammatories.

As I packed to go home, I tipped the nurse who helped me through the process. Then, heading back to the San Diego airport, my driver was stopped by border patrol. There was an issue with the van, and someone asked me for my ID. In a panic, I put one of those $100 envelopes inside my passport. They returned my ID without the cash, and I was free to cross the border with $500 to spare.

Later that day, I used the rest of my bribe money to buy a pass to the American Airlines Admiral's Club. It's been over a decade, and I've been a member ever since. *Just like the rich do it!*

THE DECISION THAT CHANGED MY LIFE

Weight-loss surgery transformed my life. If that sounds like the wrong lesson to learn in an era of feminism and fat activism—where we attack women of all sizes on Twitter and Instagram instead of expressing empathy to everyone who is on a journey of self-improvement—maybe it is.

But it's also true. I have no regrets. Nor am I ashamed of it.

When I returned to work at Pfizer after the surgery, I was unrecognizable. I didn't lose weight right away, but my face was different—less scowly, more smiley. I lost my negative attitude and felt in control of my life. Weight-loss surgery gave me a greater sense of agency, which reflected in how I carried myself. People stopped me in the hall and asked if I had been on vacation.

I was like, "Yes, I went to Mexico."

Not the entire truth, but not a total lie.

Within weeks, I stopped craving crappy food and converted to vegetarianism. I joined the local gym and began training for my first 5K. It also didn't hurt that I got myself into therapy and weaned myself off the heavy-duty antidepressants.

And soon after coming home, I had more great news: my anonymous blog caught fire. Audiences found my website while searching for terms like "my job sucks" and "I hate HR." My blog offered people hope for a better life, and hope is the antidote for being stuck.

Within six months of my surgery in Tijuana, I left Pfizer and started ghostwriting for online websites. From there, I opened up my own consulting agency and joined a prestigious management association called the Conference Board as a contributing editor to its print magazine.

o o o

All these years later, my lap band is no longer activated. It's still in my body—wrapped loosely around my stomach— but it doesn't restrict my food intake. Sometimes I think about reactivating it when my diet falls apart. But instead of cutting calories, I've learned to cut myself some slack.

When my diet suffers and I feel exhausted, or when I've stopped getting enough exercise, it's almost always because I'm not getting to bed at a decent time.

Maybe it feels ridiculous to read a story about a former HR manager with depression who finds love and self-acceptance through sketchy bariatric surgery. If it feels that way, this book isn't for you. This book is for people open to creative, and even crazy, ideas—ready to take risks and put themselves first.

My life moved forward once I stopped thinking only my job could bring me happiness. My math was backward. Exercising, eating a better quality of food, following a healthy sleep cycle, writing, starting a business, and changing my mind-set is what ultimately brought me joy. Once I put myself first, my life began to flourish. Yours will, too.

I know it's not easy to put yourself first, take control of your career, and be your own advocate. But as Barack Obama said, "Change will not come if we wait for some other person or some other time. We are the ones we've been waiting for. We are the change that we seek."

Change begins by asking hard questions about your motivation, beliefs, desires, abilities, and limitations. Why do you make the choices you make? What are your values? How can you fix the fixable and let the rest go? What else or who else are you ignoring at the expense of work?

Nobody can answer those questions for you, and you probably can't answer them alone. Do you have access to a therapist or an employee assistance program? An EAP is a resource that assists workers with addressing their health and their mental and emotional well-being. If you don't have access to an EAP or a therapist, talk to a mentor. Speak to a member of the clergy or a trusted friend. Spend some money and invest in a certified career coach. Join an online membership community with like-minded souls.

Since leaving Pfizer, I've apologized to and reconciled with many of my former colleagues and bosses. They say that life is short, even on the longest days, and I couldn't wait another minute to reconnect with people and try to understand their stories and share mine.

I've also applied the lessons that I learned at Pfizer to my consultancy, coaching countless people to stop making career and life decisions based on fear. I have helped them learn to start with small things to improve the quality of their lives. My clients come to me looking for someone else to solve their problems. But when they leave, they're fully immersed in the world of *self*-leadership. They refuse to rush into the office for early morning meetings and instead drive their kids to school every day. They sign up for memberships to the YMCA, find personal trainers, and become more mindful of their eating habits by working with nutritionists. They implement small fixes and incremental changes, conducting tiny experiments that may or may not work. That's what putting yourself first and prioritizing your emotional and physical well-being are all about.

Chuck Palahniuk, the author of *Fight Club*, once said, "People don't want their lives fixed. Nobody wants their problems solved. Their dramas. Their distractions. Their stories resolved. Their messes cleaned up. Because what would they have left? Just the big scary unknown."

You might say most people who quote Chuck Palahniuk are emotionally repressed dudes who cling to the last vestiges of youth. But hear me out: Chuck isn't entirely wrong on this one. It's easy to spend years deprioritizing your needs and focusing on distractions that don't matter than to face the big, scary unknown. But I'm here to tell you that the big scary unknown isn't all that scary.

I got budget weight-loss surgery in Tijuana so I could regain control over my life decisions and expectations— let's fix your problems before it becomes that bad for you. If you need more sleep, get it. If you need time off, take it. Claim what's yours, just like a company would do. You don't owe anyone an explanation for prioritizing self-care. Not your boss. Not your colleagues. And certainly not your friends at the office.

You fix work by fixing *yourself*. I promise—because I'm proof.

2

Be a Slacker

WORK LESS TO
ACCOMPLISH MORE

Standing on a street corner waiting for no
one is power.

—GREGORY CORSO

When you meet someone for the first time, how
do you introduce yourself? Here's what I used
to say: "Hi, my name is Laurie. I'm a writer, speaker, and
entrepreneur. I love taking on the worst parts of corporate
America and calling it out. I worked for companies like
Pfizer and Monsanto, but ultimately left the traditional
world of work at the beginning of the Great Recession to
launch my own consulting, coaching, and public speaking
firm. What do you do for a living?"

You may recognize this speech as an elevator pitch,
but it's so much more. It's a "career identity statement"

that signals information to listeners about my education, status, and standing in life. Why do we use career identity statements?

I'm not a behavioral psychologist, but I've read enough to know that the brain evolves slowly. You may think you're schmoozing with a bunch of important people at a cocktail party, but your brain is still scanning the horizon for saber-toothed tigers. The statements you make about yourself are powerful tools that help others cut through the noise and enact quick, reasonable estimates about you. They're a sort of hack to help the brain understand if you are a friend or a competitor.

Unfortunately, career identity statements can also be toxic.

First, you are more than what you do for work. A job title is a fraction of your identity. You have hopes, feelings, and dreams that can be expressed in a variety of ways. When you define yourself by your job, you limit your capacity to contribute as a partner, a caregiver, or even a community member.

Next, you might hide behind your career identity and use work to distract from trauma, abuse, or emotional chaos. It feels good to be a VP of marketing or a senior designer when life is hard. It's a signal to others that you are successful despite the odds. But your job isn't the solution to your personal problems or challenges. And no career title will ever bring you joy or purpose unless you first fix what's broken in your personal life.

Finally, comparison is the thief of joy. Career identity statements make it hard to see someone as anything other than a competitor. If you work sixty hours a week as a manager but Judy only works forty-five, shouldn't Judy be demoted? If you went to the same college as Liam but he has a company car, isn't something wrong with you?

When people work with me to improve their relationship with work, one of the first things I do is help them understand the limited usefulness of a career identity statement and then redirect their time and energy to developing identity statements about their whole lives.

I ask: What do you do when you're not working? Where is one place in the world you haven't been that's on your bucket list? If you had permission to be a slacker at work, how would you spend time each week focusing on yourself?

That last question raises a lot of objections. People tell me, "Laurie, I can't be a slacker. It's not in my DNA to do anything other than a great job. I've got a work ethic."

But I'm like: Who's the slacker? The person negatively obsessing about her job all week long while on the clock, or the person who protects her calendar and takes enough time off to be productive at work? You could work twenty-five to thirty hours a week and only give 80 percent at the office and still be more productive than more than half of the workforce who are disengaged and working not nearly as hard as you.

It's my goal to help people kill the career identity

statement in favor of a #humanstatement about who they are and what they believe in. Instead of going to a networking event and talking about work, it's time to talk about what really matters—family, friends, hobbies, and interests. And this effort starts with me. Now, this is how I introduce myself at networking events:

"Hi, my name is Laurie. I'm a writer, speaker, and entrepreneur. I once had a bullshit job in HR, but I left the traditional world of work at the beginning of the Great Recession to focus on my well-being. When I'm not working, I volunteer to foster kittens and read fiction. What do you do for fun?"

It's not perfect, but it's *human*.

It's time to work on your #humanstatement. It starts by recognizing that you are more than the sum of your job. You have an individual identity as a thinker, student, parent, partner, writer, runner, yogi, or even just a good friend who always brings cookies to parties. You are not what you do for a living. What you do for a living simply allows you to be you.

Work won't make you happy. You make you happy. It's time to deprioritize your career and instead prioritize the good stuff: relationships, community, sleeping, eating nutritious meals, and enjoying time away from the screen. What's the secret? Where's the hack to this magical, mystical life balance?

There is no quick fix, but here's my advice: be a slacker.

HOW TO BECOME A SLACKER

There's no universal definition for a slacker, but the word loosely describes a person who will do anything to avoid work.

Every family has one. Maybe it's your cousin, uncle, or sister-in-law who always asks for money and never pays you back. Or maybe it's a nephew who never has cash but always wears nice clothes and has the newest iPhone. (Not my nephews, though. They are terrific. One works as an IT professional, and the other is in elementary school.) Most families have one individual who fulfills the "kids these days" stereotype. Maybe it's you.

Every team has a slacker, too. It can be someone who comes in late, leaves early, and doesn't contribute much to a project. Sometimes it's the person who isn't overly concerned with professional relationships and does not care about the growth of a company. Work slackers are seen as opportunists who cheat the system and think they've got everybody fooled.

Slackerism was elevated to an art form in the late twentieth century with movies like *Office Space* and *The Big Lebowski*, characters like Ferris Bueller and Bart Simpson, and musicians like Kurt Cobain and Billy Corgan of the Smashing Pumpkins who told us, "The world is a vampire."

But being jaded and cynical hit a snag at the turn of the century with the onset of the global financial crisis. People couldn't afford to do anything other than *put chicken in the bucket for the man,* as Stephen Fry once wrote. Western culture also retooled itself around the birth of the social Web, the growth of interconnected communication tools, and the mass adoption of commercialized surveillance systems. It's hard to opt out of the rat race and speak your true mind when you're on Facebook and hustling for work. Companies scan your work computer and watch for sexual harassment and corporate espionage in your Slack messages. Algorithms monitor where you browse online and predict whether you're about to quit. There's even a program out there that can read your keystrokes and predict if you're at risk for suicide. Yes, really.

Speaking of the hustle, it's hard to be a slacker when our #hustleporn culture pushes you to be productive twenty-four hours a day. If you are lucky, you work for a company that gives you a work-from-home stipend to cover the cost of printer ink and pays you to freeze your eggs—but doesn't guarantee you equal pay for equal work or make your life easier when you finally unfreeze those embryos. If you are unlucky, you are a hustler who works on contract and struggles to make ends meet. And who wants to be a slacker under either of those circumstances?

Slackerism is not only frowned upon at the office, it's weaponized—especially if you're a person of color. Your well-intentioned attempt at work–life balance might be somebody else's excuse to throw you under the bus.

Now that I've painted a bleak image of slackers, let me flip the script and say that while nobody wants to be seen as the jerk with a poor work ethic, slackerism might save your soul.

○ ○ ○

Deanna is the VP of communications for a digital media organization. She worked hard throughout high school and college as a student athlete and scholar, then she went back to school as a working mom to pursue her MBA. Deanna is known for being a creative and compassionate leader. She pushes people to be their best while also leading by example, and she doesn't shy away from hard work.

Deanna is the antithesis of a slacker, but after fifteen years as a corporate executive, she felt burned out and came looking for career advice. She's an "elder millennial" who feels a little too elderly. Could I help her get off the hamster wheel and into a job that wouldn't kill her? Was it possible to keep her current level of income with a role that didn't require so much time and energy?

Before working with me, Deanna was hunting for a new job but every opportunity sounded the same: endless hours on Slack and too much time spent managing corporate politics rather than doing the fun work of innovation.

"I'm exhausted. My team can see it. My family tells me I work too much. And I can't keep taking Zoloft forever."

When I asked Deanna about her sleeping and eating habits, she laughed out loud. With two kids under the age of six—and one following her lead by showing an interest in sports—she doesn't eat or sleep well.

This was Deanna's life before COVID-19: early morning wake-ups, daycare, carpool, a long commute to and from work, little flexibility, lots of responsibility with her kids, a spouse with an executive leadership role who doesn't do dishes, and hobbies and interests that go unexplored because there aren't enough hours in the day.

"I used to do yoga and run 5Ks. Now I just participate in meetings all day long and check other people's PowerPoint decks for errors before they go to the board."

Deanna was suffering from arrival fallacy,* the feeling of disappointment you get when you reach your goals but the result isn't what you expected. Instead of being happy with your salary and enjoying your work, you ask yourself, "Is this all there is? There must be more."

There's not.

It's not uncommon to unlock the next level of your career and still feel unhappy. But it's important to know that the feelings of contentment and personal accomplishment don't come from working sixty hours and hearing "good job" from your boss. They come from confidence and maturity. You're doing great work when you solve problems, learn something new, and then spend time away

---

* https://www.forbes.com/sites/melodywilding/2016/08/22/why-reaching-your-goals-can-surprisingly-make-you-less-happy/.

from the office to support the people and activities you love.

When I suggested being a slacker to Deanna—working less, leaving early, establishing boundaries, spending time with her family, exercising, reading, and redefining what it means to be happy—she tried not to laugh again in my face.

"No offense, but people are watching me. I can't say no. They'll think I'm lazy."

I asked her to hear me out. "Since people are watching you, let's teach them something. Pretend your company is a client instead of a family. If you didn't have so much skin in the game, how would you do things differently?"

Deanna needed to learn the skill of professional detachment—staying committed to your job, doing great work, but redefining the role so it isn't your sole identity.

She didn't say no, but she didn't like it.

"This sounds risky, and I don't want to be seen as cold or disconnected."

This is a legitimate concern. Women and people of color are held to a double standard at work. They must be buttoned up but warm, savvy but deferential to the team, and data-driven yet still compassionate. Deanna told me she was always available to her team, even after business hours, which meant she wasn't present with her husband and children. It would confuse her colleagues, she argued, if she suddenly stopped answering texts in the evening without explanation.

We brainstormed ways to lock the phone up at night and discussed what it takes to create a work environment where it's safe to establish boundaries.

How could she improve daily communications but limit after-hours texting? Is it possible to track and analyze "emergencies," and work backward to create processes and behaviors that prevent them? And how could her team reach her if needed?

Deanna called a meeting and asked her team for input. Were they feeling stressed? Could they describe what it feels like to have an evening interrupted with a so-called work emergency? Deanna took the lead and shared her struggle with putting down the phone at night, and others chimed in with their stories. Soon, they all agreed that they needed common definitions for "emergency" and "work crisis."

Deanna asked her team to create a rules-of-the-road template for communicating after hours. They decided that if something was an emergency, it required a physical call. If the phone rang, and it was from a colleague, they'd try to answer the call right away or call back as soon as possible.

How did it end up working?

Deanna told me emergencies dropped 90 percent. She now has extra time to focus on her top priorities: family and personal well-being. Her evenings are free for exercise, spending time with her kids, or sitting on the couch and binge-watching TV without worrying too much about what happened at the office earlier.

Now we just need her husband to do the dishes. But I'm not a miracle worker.

"I'd be lying if I didn't admit to checking my phone in the evening," Deanna concluded. "But now I can really relax before I check my messages and get to bed."

Not only does Deanna feel more balanced and connected, but she's also taking this message to other parts of her organization. She's partnered with her local HR manager to bring the work–life balance rules to other business units and teams within the company. Just recently, Deanna spoke on a panel at a leadership conference and sang the praises of professional detachment, honest communication, and personal accountability for well-being.

Professional detachment—the act of pausing, reflecting, and treating your job like a puzzle to solve instead of an extension of your identity—saved Deanna from leaving her company. She hasn't labeled herself as a slacker, but I'll do it for her. And you, too.

I'm thinking of making T-shirts.

BEAT THE SLUMP

Marcus was a seasoned human resources leader about two weeks away from a nervous breakdown.

When I worked with Marcus, he was an energetic HR manager with a passion for labor relations who called me "Munchkin." Now he was a middle-aged mid-level director with two kids, lots of gray hair, and a spare tire around his tummy. It had only been a few years, but he looked much older and very, very tired.

We grabbed a booth at a quintessentially Chicago restaurant called the Golden Nugget and caught up on the basics over a stack of pancakes. Before they served the food, Marcus explained that he was recently diagnosed with type 2 diabetes and excused himself to check his blood sugar level. It shocked me. I knew that the number of adults with type 2 diabetes was increasing in most countries,* but I didn't understand how my friend—who seemed healthy just a few years before—could have a serious condition formerly reserved for people like my elderly grandmother?

When he left the table, I almost cried. My friend was in a slump.

The slump gets us all from time to time in our careers. Have you ever worked your ass off and felt like nobody noticed? Has your boss ever told you to do a better job managing up? Does your health take a backseat to your long commute? Was there a moment in your career when you felt helpless and stuck?

That's the slump. It affects the body and the mind. It's brutal on both the ego and the soul.

Marcus came back to the table and said, "Laurie, I'm thinking about going out on my own."

Like a consulting company?

---

* https://www.idf.org/aboutdiabetes/what-is-diabetes/facts-figures.html.

"Yeah, a consulting company focused on delivering real-life diversity and inclusion solutions to small-to medium-size organizations. I'll do a little coaching, a little speaking, and whatever it takes to get started."

I was speechless. Leave a job with health insurance and benefits when you're newly diagnosed with an illness? That was the opposite of what he should do.

"You're giving me a face, Munchkin. What's up?" (It's true. I don't have a poker face.)

I fundamentally believe that quitting your job and becoming a consultant is almost always bad. And yes, I did it. That's how I know it's a bad idea. Here's why. A corporate consultant isn't just a consultant. He's a corporate officer, full-time administrator, bookkeeper, travel agent, sales leader, revenue officer, head of marketing, social media consultant, customer service agent, and intern in those moments when you run to Staples because you're out of ink and need to print a proposal.

Consulting can be lonely. Even if you're a burned-out introvert who dreams of working from home, you'll spend more time in your head than with other people. The change from an open-office environment to your upstairs office above the kitchen can be abrupt.

New business owners have rarely saved enough money. To quit your job and become a consultant, you'll need the equivalent of two to three years' worth of cash flow in your savings account to sustain the initial launch and growth of your company. Also, you must live without your old corporate benefits or replace those perks. When I worked at Pfizer, the company offered extensive private medical coverage with comprehensive prescription drug benefits. The retirement plan was generous, and my department paid for my mobile phone and home Internet. When I wasn't feeling great, we had a health clinic with no copays and access to well-being programs. Plus, all of my office supplies were free.

Moreover, the tax system in most countries doesn't favor small businesses. It promotes the interests of historically wealthy people who own property and earn their income through the work of others. Across the world, there is nothing about late-stage capitalism that supports small and local companies over big conglomerates.

And getting people to write a check is hard. Your new corporate customer has never run a small business, does not know how important their company's money is to your bottom line, and wants to nickel-and-dime you to death because it makes them feel like a baller to negotiate.

Corporate burnout is real, but quitting your job because you're in a slump is a terrible idea that might make your life worse. You can only fix work by fixing yourself, not by running to the gig economy for solutions. Whatever is broken about your life won't heal if your paycheck dries up, and life doesn't get easier when you're under the pressure of launching a new business and asked to attend every local book club or Rotary meeting because they need a local thought leader who will speak for free.

I told Marcus, "Please don't quit your job. Let's pull back on work as much as possible without getting fired. Then we'll work on a plan to identify three things that are driving you crazy but are within your reach to fix. We can take baby steps and write a business plan on the side. If my solutions don't work, then I'll help you launch a company."

He thanked me for the offer to help and assured me he was thinking about my advice. Then he quit his job a week later and announced on LinkedIn he was hanging a shingle as an HR consultant.

Do I really need to tell you how this panned out? Marcus spent the better part of two years trying to launch that consulting company while feeling completely unwell. He started a blog, spoke at some conferences, and even appeared on a few podcasts. I ran into him twice. Once, he seemed okay and even happy. But the next time I saw him, maybe ten months later, he asked if I could help him find a job back in corporate human resources.

It turns out that Marcus had exhausted his savings and the patience of his wife. He was spending too much time on the computer competing with other "thought leaders" for likes and retweets, and not enough time converting leads in his sales funnel. His health hadn't improved, either.

When I asked him what kind of job he wanted, Marcus told me, "Something with a paycheck that won't kill me."

Oh boy, I know that feeling. Every consultant has a moment where we wonder, "Why did I quit my job? Was it so bad? I should have shut my mouth and sucked it up."

Marcus needed help, but there was no way he would find a job without doing some inner work to fix that initial slump. So I promised him I'd help with the job search if he would do a few things for me.

First, I asked him to return to the doctor and get a physical. We needed to know if Marcus was in a slump for *biological*, *psychological*, or *environmental* reasons. Medicine fixes biology, therapy fixes psychology, and coaching fixes the environmental reasons we make the same career mistakes repeatedly.

Next, I asked Marcus to wear a Fitbit or some device to track his steps and ensure he wasn't spending his days sitting at his desk waiting for job offers that would never appear. It didn't matter if he hit the much-lauded ten thousand steps, but he had to do something other than check his email all day long. Stepping-tracking is a good old-fashioned accountability tool.

Also, nobody takes over the world on three hours of sleep, so we tracked his sleep, too, and had a goal of seven hours of rest each night.

Finally, Marcus had to schedule in more time for fun. I didn't care if he read, took up dancing, or spent more time with his kids. He just needed to get off the Internet and shift gears.

Marcus agreed to my terms, and we got to work. I introduced him to recruiters in my network who had experience finding jobs for returning workers and mature candidates. We had to manage the expectations of hiring managers (who are often ageist), along with Marcus's expectations to earn more than his old salary. We stayed off job boards, which are useless for people over the age of forty. And we dissected his network on LinkedIn for connections that could open doors.

Finally, Marcus and I spoke at great length about his attitude and expectations for the next job. He's not a traditional slacker and wants to give everything 110 percent. But what if he didn't need to work that hard? I made my case for being a slacker.

"What if you gave your best 72 percent and saved the rest for your family and your personal life?"

Marcus paused and said, "Maybe."

Marcus is now working in a job that wasn't too dissimilar from his last one. The title is the same, the input and outputs are nearly identical, and his salary and bonus structure match what he earned in previous roles. But we did the important work of improving his health outcomes, elevating his mood, and finding him a job that wouldn't eat his soul alive. And he realized that if you build a better system for yourself and invest in your well-being, the system you work in doesn't matter. Fix yourself. Then bring all that goodness in your personal life to work. A healthy lifestyle and realigned priorities will help you triumph over the mediocre obligations of an ordinary job.

This is good advice for you, too. Focus on being the best version of you. Work with integrity. Be professionally detached. And most of all, be a slacker.

WHAT THE HELL IS SELF-CARE?

A few years ago, my husband and I went to couples' counseling to fine-tune our marriage. Every marriage has challenges, and our relationship is no different. Ken is a saver, I'm a spender. He's guarded, I'm energetic. Ken loves cats, but I want a menagerie of animals including a dog, some chickens, and a few baby goats. These aren't irreconcilable differences. Our goal with counseling was simple: we loved each other and wanted to communicate more effectively.

One of my girlfriends recommended a counselor who'd recently moved to the area where we live. Ken went for a solo visit and was asked about his self-care habits.

Ken asked, "What habits?"

The counselor replied, "Self-care."

Ken needed the counselor to define self-care because, as a PhD chemical engineer who leads a global team of other technical people, he had truly never heard the phrase. She told him, "Self-care is many things: exercise, nutrition, creativity, and sleep. What are you doing to take care of yourself?"

When Ken came home and told me he didn't know the meaning of self-care, I thought he'd had a stroke.

"How do you not know what self-care means?"

He said, "I don't read Goop."

I asked, "What do you think it means?"

He blushed and said, "I thought she was talking about masturbation."

For once in my life, I was silent.

"She also asked about my parents," Ken continued. "I thought that's how it goes: childhood, masturbation, and then dreams." (Not gonna lie, that's a solid overview of most therapy sessions.)

In retrospect, it's not surprising that Ken wasn't aware of the self-care craze. True self-care, at its core, is a simple idea: prioritize your well-being. In short, this means: be a slacker, slow down, and stop trying to keep up with the Joneses because, ultimately, the only thing that matters is your health. Because of social conditioning, it's a message that doesn't resonate with middle-age corporate dudes like my husband, although it should, because those are the individuals who report the highest rates of despair, depression, and disengagement.

I remain wholly supportive of healthy self-care routines and rituals, but the concept itself has become twisted. If you watch YouTube videos and Instagram stories, self-care no longer means wellness. It means purchasing exotic beauty items from former celebrities turned gurus to mask the pain in your soul, stocking up on new clothes to signal to your peers that you're evolved, and following the latest guru peddling candles, bath products, and other stuff you don't need that will only make her company richer.

When Facebook serves me ads for facial creams and massage therapy devices, I want to shake my fists and yell at the clouds. Self-care in the twenty-first century is tantamount to fraud. It's a thin veneer of self-acceptance that masks a deeper corporate message of unworthiness that can only be vanquished through consumption. Contemporary self-care is trash.

There is no way that drinking coconut oil coffee or using a motorized brush to remove dead skin cells will improve the overall condition of your life. And what's worse are those meditation and relaxation apps on your phone that promise happiness in under eight minutes. While the science behind mindfulness is strong, there's no reliable data behind the efficacy of those apps.

But we live in a world with a singular message: if you can buy it, you can become it. Peace, love, and enlightenment are just a click away on your mobile device.

Our world is also full of contradictions: We're supposed to go slowly and eat natural foods without toxins or pesticides, but most of our employers amp up the pace of work and don't pay us enough to afford healthy, organic produce. We're meant to get sunshine and exercise, but very few can afford to take time off work and book a hiking excursion to Sedona or a beach trip to the Caribbean. And they tell us to take care of our bodies and get enough sleep, but our system of work continually demands greater productivity and more time on the job.

The self-care economy is a house of cards built on monetizing your fear, shame, and ignorance in the most treacherous of ways: by *pretending* to care about you. They know you feel bad because they made you feel bad. And now they're swooping in with a solution that doesn't fix anything.

I'm jealous of my husband for not knowing that this micro-economy existed. What a wonderful world, not to know about collagen supplements and membership-based communities that will help you get seven-minute abs.

But now you (and my husband) are aware that the self-care industry exists to make you feel bad, and you have an obligation to fight back via feeling good on your own. How can you be a slacker and prioritize emotional and physical well-being without spending a dime?

Well, you need sleep. Fresh air. Nutritious food. Physical movement. Time away from the Internet. More time with your family. Hobbies and interests. Community endeavors where you connect with people. Opportunities to perform acts of service and be helpful. And it never hurts to adopt some animals.

Is it that easy? Hell no! Life is hard. You will still suffer. You will compromise. You might even feel dissatisfied with your progress and need to go to Tijuana to fix your shit. But at least you'll be suffering on your terms and without accruing compounding interest on consumer credit cards that keep you stuck in your unsatisfying job.

If you don't know where to find all that healthy living and cheap self-care on your own—or you can't see yourself developing a new hobby at your age—then do nothing at first. Just watch the successful people around you. When you feel like it, start small. Find someone who is living the life you want. Befriend them and be curious. Ask questions. Copy what you like about their life and discard the rest.

I had a colleague at Pfizer named Tim who was living the life I wanted: respected by his peers, detached from his job but mature enough to deliver excellent results unencumbered by work drama and political shenanigans. He rarely worked nights and weekends. He and his wife, Vanessa, lived simply and took long vacations. His life was so fantastic, I thought it was a lie.

When I got to know him a little better, I learned that the life he built—of balance, interconnectedness with his partner, and financial security—wasn't always perfect and took years to develop. His career narrative was like mine and yours: worked a few jobs, hated them, looked internally, and realized that he had to fix work by fixing himself.

Tim still sometimes hates work, he told me. He took classes in anger management because his job was so frustrating, then enrolled in a course on mindfulness-based stress reduction. From there, he went back and received a coaching certificate. To this day, he still struggles with the very human tendency to react before he thinks.

"I'm not a poster child for work–life balance," he said. "It just looks like I have my life under control because so many other people don't."

After I returned from Tijuana, I told Tim about my surgery and asked for advice. I had been toying with leaving my job and becoming a writer. My blog was doing well. I had savings in the bank that would allow for quitting my job. But I was still hesitant to take a risk and bet on myself.

"This job will eat me alive if I let it. Should I stay or go?"

"You should talk to an expert about what's going on in your life," he replied. "And stop looking to other people, especially me, for answers to questions that only you can answer."

That's when I told Tim, "But I think you're the most normal guy I know."

Tim laughed. "What? Me? No, I'm a *slacker*. Haven't you been listening?"

I was listening. And I hope you're listening, too.

Work on crafting an identity that's bigger than your job. Look internally for answers instead of buying a solution in the beauty aisle. Be a slacker and put yourself first. It might seem risky, but, man, is it worth it.

3

Bet on Yourself

BEAT IMPOSTOR SYNDROME
AND BELIEVE
YOUR OWN HYPE

I have just realized that the stakes are myself
I have no other ransom money, nothing to
break or barter but my life.

—DIANE DI PRIMA

When I was little, there was no grand plan for my future. My dad often joked around that I would be a flight attendant because I had straight teeth, while my mom hoped I'd marry well despite the fact that this was the opposite of her feminist instincts. There were no Mandarin language classes, college exam preparatory classes, or after-school activities.

When I finally went to college, I didn't declare a major until my junior year. I thought about specializing in law, psychology, women's studies, and even theology before finally choosing a degree in English. I didn't know it at the time, but I was a generalist: someone interested in a lot of things but with no real expertise in one specific field.

The risk of being a generalist is that you're unfocused and late to the game. My choice to study English and creative writing—with an emphasis on writers like William Burroughs, Jack Kerouac, Nikki Giovanni, and Charles Bukowski—didn't put me into a graduate program where I would emerge with solid career options. Instead, it inadvertently put me down the not-so-fabulous path of being an HR manager, figuring out how to use Excel like the rest of humankind.

But the benefit of being a generalist is that I had an education rooted in the humanities, where I studied art, drama, romance, and heartache. When I fell into human resources, I had the human part down. And by comparison, employment law and hiring methodologies were much easier to learn.

David Epstein, author of the bestseller *Range: Why Generalists Triumph in a Specialized World*, believes we can help our children become successful in their future careers by encouraging them to sample an array of life experiences without the pressure to master any specific task. Show them different media, play them multiple genres of music, expose them to a wide assortment of art, introduce them to a variety of sports, and encourage diverse friendships. The wider the range of experiences, the better your kids are at thriving in the new economy.

It's not too late for adults, either. Epstein encourages his readers to broaden their horizons and gain exposure to diverse experiences. Don't be myopic and pick one thing—like your job, career, family, or passion. Pick lots of things, and you'll become better at the one core thing you love.

Whether you have a specialized or generalist skill set, there's one hard-and-fast rule in HR: you won't know if a career suits you until you try it. Many people start out with plans to do one thing but wind up in a completely different world. Lawyer. Accountant. Industrial designer. Very few of us have a straightforward path.

Instead, when you fall into a job, no matter the reason, the result is a "happenstance career."

Did you plan to be an actress but wind up in pharmaceutical sales? Were you dreaming of life as a teacher but found yourself working a corporate job to pay your bills? Did you go to school for journalism but land as a volleyball coach at the YMCA instead?

Welcome to having a happenstance career.

If you just wound up in your job, know this: you're not alone. There's a long tradition of tumbling headfirst into a career or industry. There are no solid numbers on what percentage of the population has a happenstance career, but the world needs talented people who fell into jobs like a phlebotomist, library clerk, and luggage handler. We need accounts payable managers, warehouse workers, and customer service representatives. If you are helpful, your job matters. All work is important and dignified when it's rooted in service, regardless of whether or not you planned for your career.

Happenstance careers can be as great or as miserable as any other path. People love a job that offers great pay, benefits, flexibility, and the opportunity to pursue outside interests. But it feels rotten when the boss is a jerk and the mood is negative. And it's worse when the atmosphere is toxic and nobody cares about the workers' well-being. In those instances, it doesn't matter if someone planned for that career or not.

Let me repeat: if you're stuck in a job that eats at your soul, it doesn't have to stay that way. Are you bold and brave? Do you take risks and voice your concerns? Would you raise your hand in a meeting to share your thoughts?

Or do you leave your job every day with mixed emotions because you didn't say the things you wanted to? Are you enduring bullshit from coworkers because you're waiting for your kids to go to college—or the magical milestone of retirement, whatever the hell that is? Have you considered following a dream or taking a risk but stopped yourself because you think it will fail?

There is no change without loss, no dream without risk. Don't blow opportunities to move forward in life because you're waiting for a sign to take a risk and bet on yourself.

This is your sign. The time is now.

TAKE A F**KING RISK

My buddy Scott Stratten is a keynote speaker, marketing expert, and master of the happenstance career. After graduating from Sheridan University in Ontario, Scott went to work as an HR generalist at the Goodwill in Toronto.

If you think your career sucks, Scott managed employee relations for thrift store workers and once caught an employee stealing from the cash register.

As Scott pointed out, "If you're stealing from Goodwill, you're going straight to hell."

Scott tried to press charges against the worker, but the employees' union countersued for illegal termination. Because he has integrity, Scott was determined to see this dismissal through to the bitter end. However, Scott's boss told him to give the employee a settlement to make him go away.

Scott was furious and turned it down.

His boss said, "Do you want to call the president of our nonprofit and tell him why we had to spend an extra $20,000 in legal fees when you could have settled it for $5,000?"

Scott said, "It's the principle."

The boss looked at Scott and said, "There's no such thing."

In that moment, Scott knew this job wouldn't allow him to flourish, and he almost quit on the spot. But instead of having a sanctimonious meltdown, he identified a career goal and worked backward to reverse engineer the risks and make his dreams come true.

How did he do it?

Scott always knew he wanted to be like his hero Les Brown, a motivational speaker. It was his dream to travel around the world, deliver keynote speeches, and change lives. But you can't go from HR manager to Tony Robbins–level motivator in a blink of an eye, and Scott dabbled in a few other businesses to test his mettle as an entrepreneur.

Very few people are successful on their first go-around at anything, and Scott was no exception. After several years, Scott found his businesses in a slump, and bored by the slow momentum, he became curious about the world around him.

"I thought, 'What is this Twitter thing? Let me try it out and see how it goes.' In January 2009, I tweeted 7,000 times in a month, and I went from 1,000 followers to 10,000 followers. There's something here, I realized. And like anything in business, it's due to luck, timing, and skill."

I asked Scott to expand on how building an online presence helped him get closer to his end goal of being a speaker.

"Nobody can make waves for you," he said. "A publisher approached me and asked, 'Why haven't you written a book yet?' And I replied, 'Why haven't you offered me a book deal yet?' 'Touché,' they said."

Scott wrote his book, but he describes it as a train

wreck of forty thousand terrible words. A follower on Twitter named Alison heard about the book, volunteered to revise it, and turned his manuscript into sixty thousand polished words.

Then he married her.

Scott and Alison Stratten are now the coauthors of six business books, co-owners of UnMarketing Inc., and cohosts of the UnPodcast. They have five children between them, two dogs, and two cats. Scott fulfilled his dream of developing a career like Les Brown's and was inducted into the CPAE Speaker Hall of Fame in 2018.

But he will be the first to admit his dreams didn't come true overnight, and yours won't, either.

Sure, you may not want to quit your job and become a public speaker, but you probably dream of achieving other goals, such as more accountability and responsibility at work.

No matter what, it starts by taking a risk and betting on yourself.

You can't close the gap between "who you are" and "who you want to be" without getting quiet, homing in on your personality and preferences, and really discovering who you are inside and out.

So, tell me, who are you? What's your risk profile?

GREEN: You make bold moves without blinking an eye because you have done your homework and know what's up. No matter the environment or circumstances, you've got this. You have the confidence and emotional intelligence to walk into a room of strangers and accomplish the goals you put forward. If it doesn't work out, you're not afraid of Plan B. And when you name the people you admire, The Rock, Michelle Obama, and Matthew McConaughey are your spirit animals.

YELLOW: You are a moderate risk-taker who can command the stage and handle an elevated heartbeat but still remain humble. You think before you speak, and it's okay if your goals take longer to reach. You prefer small steps and incremental change to blowing things up and taking charge amid chaos. Your celebrity matches are Stephen Colbert, Tina Fey, and Denzel Washington. (I'm sure there are some younger international stars out there, but I'm Gen X and American. The only celebrity who matters to me is Keanu Reeves.)

RED: You are analytical to the extreme. You can't take a risk without examining the pros and cons from every angle—and maybe not even then. You take chances only after thinking long and hard about what's going down, and you see yourself reflected in Marlin from *Finding Nemo* and Sheldon Cooper from *The Big Bang Theory*.

○ ○ ○

Where do you fall? Are you on top of your game? Somewhere in the middle, stuck in the mud and finding it impossible to advance toward your goals? Whatever your risk profile, I know one thing is true: it's time to place a bet on yourself.

THE PREMORTEM WILL SAVE YOUR SOUL

I have a mentor named Chris Ostoich. He's the cofounder and head of innovation at LISNR, a company that creates a new way to transmit data using sound. Chris and his team have raised millions of dollars in venture capital and serve customers like Ticketmaster, Jaguar Land Rover, Visa, and Lenovo.

Chris is living his best Michelle Obama life.

Back in 2016, Chris and I chatted about risk, failure, and betting on yourself. He mentioned the Space Shuttle *Challenger* flight. If you weren't alive, let me fill you in. In January 1986, seven astronauts died when the shuttle exploded right after liftoff. One person on board was America's first teacher in space, which is how I wound up watching the tragedy unfold with my fellow sixth graders at St. Wenceslaus Catholic school on the northwest side of Chicago. We tuned in to the local NBC affiliate to support the historic milestone. But when the space shuttle exploded, the room fell silent. Someone finally spoke and said, "Maybe they ejected? Are they floating in the ocean?"

The nuns made us say prayers.

Chris and I reflected on the horror of that explosion and talked about how NASA retooled its entire approach to preflight communication after the accident. It turns out an engineer named Bob Ebeling* predicted the space

---

* https://www.npr.org/sections/thetwo-way/2016/03/21/470870426/challenger-engineer-who-warned-of-shuttle-disaster-dies.

shuttle would explode. He tried to prevent it, but his bosses didn't listen. For years, Bob blamed himself. It was only later in life that he could finally forgive himself for the mistakes of others at work.

Chris and I reflected on this tragedy and wondered what it would take for people to stop making mistakes at work. Some teams do postmortems after projects, but nobody is ever brave enough to flash forward and think about how projects might fail in the future. People communicate poorly, won't take risks for fear of failure, and make crucial mistakes because of organizational politics. Nobody likes conflict, which means the person who kisses ass best is rewarded the most.

Work improves when everybody on a team aligns around a shared set of expectations but remains brave and courageous enough to challenge the status quo as necessary. Work could be transformed if leaders had an instrument that allowed people to raise their hands—anonymously or otherwise—and share glitches before projects fail.

Chris asked, "Have you ever heard of the premortem?"

I had not. And I'm guessing neither have you.

Before you do anything—paint your kitchen, design a website, build a new bridge, enter data into a spreadsheet—pause and reflect. Think about how you will fail before you fail. Then work backward to create solutions for this hypothetical failure and put those action points into your project plan.

For example, let's say you're video conferencing with

your parents this weekend. We know the many ways it can go wrong. Somebody might talk about politics. Your mother or father might criticize your life choices. You might drink too much on your side of the screen. Things that should remain unsaid might be said, and your parents might hold a grudge for a very long time.

If you can see the failure now, you can beat it. Develop a plan and implement a strategy. That's the premortem.

Variations of the premortem have been around forever, but its popularity did not take off in earnest until Dr. Gary Klein introduced the methodology to readers of *Harvard Business Review* in the early 2000s. Today, it is used by Fortune 100 companies, small-to-medium-size businesses, and consultants around the world. According to research, your chances of success improve by over 30 percent if you attempt to predict failure before starting and change your behaviors and actions in order to avoid it.*

When Chris finished explaining the logic behind the premortem, I almost fell over.

If you come from a dysfunctional family, you've most likely mastered the art of solving problems before they happen. Whether you call it a premortem or worst-case-scenario thinking, the idea isn't new. Does your stepfather tend to come home from work in a bad mood? Is money tight at the end of the month? Do your parents argue after a night out drinking? Children quickly learn to anticipate

---

* https://hbr.org/2007/09/performing-a-project-premortem.

what might go wrong and change their behavior to proactively avoid triggering the surrounding adults.

And at work, you have probably learned to avoid similar minefields. Is a manager bullying his direct report? Stay out of his way. Does the receptionist always show up to work in a see-through top? Don't let your gaze fall below her chin. Need to attend sexual harassment and active shooter training? Keep your head low, say nothing, and it will be over quickly.

People use the premortem every single day without having a name for it, imagining what could go wrong and making contingency plans.

I asked Chris, "Has anybody turned this into an app?"

"I don't know," he said. "But if it's possible, you're the woman for the job."

My life changed in an instant, and I went from blogger to tech founder. Chris and I cofounded a company called GlitchPath, which told people, "We are here to help you beat failure."

Because it's just that easy!

BLIND SPOTS AND FAILURE ARE REAL

When someone launches a start-up, the pressure is on to have confidence without swagger. The marketplace wants a founder who delivers flawless product and rock-solid user experience while remaining professionally detached enough to take feedback and criticism along the way. And if you're like me and promise to help people beat failure, you'd better not fail.

Chris brought on two employees to help launch GlitchPath: a designer and a full stack engineer. They were coworkers in Cincinnati who had been toying around with an idea to beat failure, too. I was the missing piece—a woman who knew how to design a business plan and sell it to investors. I found a tech adviser named William Tincup to round out our team of five. GlitchPath team was born.

The good news is that we didn't have any stereotypical young millennials on our team—kids who wear noise-canceling headphones, want a trophy for everything, and demand avocado toast in the cafeteria—because that stereotype doesn't exist. If young tech workers were actually bratty and entitled children in hoodies, business would never get done.

But the bad news is that everybody on our team was super busy. Three of us were parents, two were entrepreneurs who led their own companies, and all of us worked long hours. We knew the risks of launching a tech company: nine out of ten start-ups fail, due in large part to poor communication, and women-owned companies face even more difficulties at the beginning, receiving less funding on average from investors.*

Except for me, everyone had another full-time job. I was the only one with a portfolio career, which meant

---

* https://carta.com/blog/why-women-get-less-funding/.

that I juggled several part-time writing and marketing gigs while also out on the road giving speeches to HR audiences. Right away our work wasn't equally distributed. We made little progress as a group because GlitchPath wasn't a priority for my colleagues. In fact, one guy missed several important meetings for softball practice. Seriously.

Being a woman in technology is tough, and I legitimately struggled to find my voice as a leader. When I led meetings, my tone fell somewhere between mom and stone-cold bitch. But the thing about running a tech company is that your voice doesn't matter when you have metrics, calendars, and your own two eyes and a mouth to call out bullshit. Our team missed deadlines and it was unacceptable.

The other problem was that nobody would use the premortem to assess failure within our own team. I finally caught on to the idea that we should drink our own champagne and asked my colleagues to take a premortem on product challenges or roadblocks.

I asked, "Why can't we launch our own website? Why is the interface of our product all jacked up? Before we throw more time and money at a problem, let's do a premortem and understand *why* we're failing."

The more I pressed my colleagues, the more they resisted. I learned that my team loved the premortem for other people but not for themselves.

It was an important insight into our product but an

inconvenient truth for our team. Having already spent several thousand dollars on travel and team meetings with no progress to show for it, my team hopped on a video call for an important discussion. I asked if we were serious about bringing GlitchPath to the market. I challenged the team to commit to following through on our assigned work and meeting deadlines for our product and website launch.

They couldn't do it, so I dissolved the company on the spot.

How could I kill GlitchPath in an instant? Easily. We hadn't formalized the corporation because one of my colleagues never signed the incorporating documents. No official paperwork meant GlitchPath was nothing more than a thought experiment. My checkbook was closed.

Actually, that's not true.

I tried to make GlitchPath work on my own—and spent my remaining budget on consultants, advisers, and outsourced design and engineering help—but a tech company only works with a team and a technical cofounder.

GlitchPath followed the path of so many start-ups and died an inglorious death due to a lack of commitment, poor team cohesion, and broken means of communication. Ultimately, the premortem didn't predict our failure because we didn't use it.

I'm not about to let you make the same mistake.

HOW TO DO A PREMORTEM CORRECTLY

You can't fix work if you don't have goals.

The premortem is an awesome tool, but it's impossible to beat failure unless you know what you want out of life. Goal setting doesn't have to be an overly arduous or complex task. Let's start with the basics. Ask yourself: *What's missing from your daily life? What do you want from a job? What do you want when no one is looking?*

Do that right now. Write down your secret dreams.

When I ask my clients to envision the future and lay out their honest goals, I'm often met with a lot of nos. No, I can't push for a promotion at work because I'm too busy with the kids and there aren't enough hours in the day. No, I can't quit my job and be an entrepreneur because I'll fail and end up homeless. No, I can't go back to school because I'm bad at math.

What a bunch of nonsense.

Goal setting is daunting because it's hard to be genuine and ask for what you want. It's much easier to make excuses and fail before you start. Most of us are telling ourselves stories based on outdated ways of how we perceive ourselves. If you still see yourself through the lens of your parents or a failed relationship, it's impossible to construct goals for a healthy and successful future.

I'm not one of those HR managers who gets off on using stupid acronyms like OKR and MBO—which mean *objectives and key results* and *management by objectives*, respectively—but goal setting is the foundation of a successful life. So before you do a premortem, take a stab and list what you want from a job, what's missing in your current environment, and what you picture in your secret dreams.

Now that you've done that, let's do a premortem and figure out how to achieve some of our goals to fix work. Ready?

First, grab the list of secret dreams you just wrote. Turn off your phone, close your eyes, and see yourself as a badass individual who pursues what she wants and won't take no for an answer. Set a timer for two minutes and imagine you failed at achieving your secret dreams. You risked it all and bombed. You were fired, humiliated, shamed, and defeated. List all the silly, ridiculous, rational, and irrational ways that you have failed. When the timer goes off, stop writing and review the list.

What you have before you is a pathway to success. Address those fears you've listed and you have the beginning of a road map to achieving your goals.

The premortem is an awesome method for helping you think through anything: angling for a promotion, starting a business, going on a family vacation, or even remodeling your home.

That's right, you can use the premortem for home improvement. My husband and I were thinking about renovating our kitchen, but the premortem quickly showed that I have trouble sticking to a budget. So, ten years later, we still have the same kitchen. Whenever we want a luxury dining experience, we go out to a fancy restaurant and don't worry about our cabinets, countertops, or appliances.

The premortem is about highlighting failure and beating it. If you want to keep your job but feel stuck or overwhelmed, let's figure out how your job fails you daily, then flip it and reverse it. Identify what's within your power to change. List your healthy rituals or habits that you'd like to incorporate into your lifestyle. Try something new like canceling unnecessary meetings to focus on the tasks that matter.

If you want to look for a job in a tightly knit industry but are afraid your boss will find out, let's figure out a plan for a confidential job search. It's not that hard. Millions of people switch jobs every day without burning bridges and ruining relationships with former employers. Let's stop wasting time and focus on potential roles that align with what you want from life and your career.

If you fear being homeless if you follow your entrepreneurial dreams, let's test the limits of how you may fail. Are you someone who would follow your passion and forget to pay your mortgage? Of course not. You've never missed a mortgage payment, so let's create a plan that incorporates your financial discipline while also allowing you to dream a little.

In all these cases, the premortem is a powerful tool to pause, reflect, and place a bet on yourself. It's a phenomenal device that gives you the mental space and time to take risks and improve your chances of success. And it's one of the few business tools that is free.

You don't need a coach, a leadership guru, or even an author to help you overcome obstacles and reach your goals—and you sure as hell don't need an app called GlitchPath. All you need is to ditch the learned helplessness and self-limited thinking that have held you back all these years.

Be brave. Be bold. Be courageous. But also be smart and do the premortem beforehand.

BURN IT ALL DOWN

Sometimes it feels like the only way to fix our lives is by burning everything down to the ground, overlooking the people and opportunities around us to make small, positive, meaningful changes.

My friend Jason Lauritsen is an author and consultant who helps companies improve employee morale and working conditions. The irony is that Jason doesn't enjoy being an employee. Every time he has a real job with a boss and corporate benefits, he's miserable. But Jason is just like you and me—an adult with obligations. And a few times in his life he's stepped back and found a "real job" to pay the bills.

Once I asked him, "Why do you think work sucks so much, and why do you hate it?"

"First I would say, I love to work," Jason responded. "I don't love working for other people."

That's fair. Autonomy and self-determination are common reasons why people start their own companies. Jason prefers to control his own destiny. I get it.

"Most people are, at a minimum, in a loveless marriage with work," Jason added. "At worst, they're in an abusive, terrible situation. And HR doesn't make it better. They build human resources systems and programs for productivity, not community. Everybody's running the same damn playbook. If you get brave and quit your job and go to another company, nothing is different."

My career as a human resources leader tells me that Jason is right. While HR has good intentions, most jobs suck, and your local HR lady can't do anything about it. Her job probably stinks, too.

But you're never on your own if you learn to appreciate the relationships and opportunities already present in your life. Look around. Things may not be as bad as they feel.

Jason said, "Do a little of what you love on the side. Maybe it's a side hustle, maybe it's teaching dance, or maybe it's coaching or reffing."

Reffing?

"Yeah, I have a friend who acts as a referee at kids' basketball because he loves basketball and wants to be connected with it. He keeps his full-time job, but the activities outside work balance the job out."

If you're still not convinced, and feel you're stuck or paralyzed by fear, there are options.

"Taking a risk doesn't mean quitting your job," Jason continued. "There's power in just doing something. If you're stuck, pick any action and do something. Update your résumé, put aside two hours and read, or go volunteer. Forward momentum in any direction will help you feel unstuck. And, once you get unstuck, opportunities show up."

Work on fixing yourself and your mental attitude; then fixing work will naturally come next. Bet on yourself as a person, an individual, a parent, a sister, a member of your community, or a volunteer. While it's important to visualize the end state of your career, it's also important to focus on the means by which you accomplish your goals.

That's why I love Jason's advice to start small, recalibrate, and try new things without letting go of a paycheck. Those efforts will pay dividends in your life—and your career—down the road.

Another way to bet on yourself is by finding community and drawing strength in numbers. My friend Amanda Hite is the founder of BTC Revolution, a social media marketing agency based in Washington, D.C. She's a talented entrepreneur and public speaker, but her former bosses haven't always appreciated her brilliance. Early in her career, a supervisor told her to hide her sexuality if she wanted to get promoted.

"You can have this job as long as you don't talk to

anybody about your lifestyle," Amanda's boss told her. Living an authentic life was out of the question.

No one would blame Amanda if she told her boss to take that promotion and shove it. Instead, she kept the job for a while, honed her business skills, and eventually built a marketing agency that hires social do-gooders to create change in the world.

I asked Amanda for advice about betting on yourself while still working in a stressful and toxic environment. Her answer was simple: get on the Internet and find community. People are forming communities everywhere, so find the people who can lift you up and offer advice during turbulent times.

"If you are an LGBT person of faith and you're in the rural Deep South, and you feel like nobody else is like you, social media provides a place for you to find others like you," Amanda said. "Beautiful things can happen online. The same is true if you have an illness or a disability, or if you're marginalized at work and need to find an ally. Social media gives you a chance to get connected."

Amanda is, clearly, an optimist. I'm a cynic and believe much of the Internet is a cesspool of stupidity and hate. How, I wondered, do you find these kindred spirits who help you bet on yourself?

Here are a few ways. Search for networking groups on LinkedIn. Join a Facebook community. Look for relevant hashtags on Twitter. Open an account and lurk on Reddit, or start a thread—also called a discussion—and ask a question. Head over to Quora and answer someone's question. Write a post on a website called Medium about your experience at work. Find a blogger who wrote something interesting and leave a comment.

You're not the first person to struggle with your job, and you're not the last person to ever wonder if it's safe to take a risk. Don't burn everything down in a fury. Raise your hand online, ask for support, and follow the advice of those who fought a similar battle and lived to tell the tale.

And if you want to bet on yourself but can't leave your job just yet? Be like my friend Sarah, who worked in human resources but had a passion for project management. She asked herself, how am I going to achieve this goal? And then she worked backward, identifying potential obstacles to career advancement before going on to pursue her PMP (Project Management Professional) Certification through the PMI (Project Management Institute). Today, she is the chief of staff for the CEO and executive leadership team at her company.

Or follow the lead of James, a chemist who works for an agency that monitors air pollution. He reached the top of his pay band and the HR department refused to give him any additional raises or promotions. James contacted me, and we did a premortem to determine if he should quit his job and bet on himself.

But James liked his company and his colleagues. He was just bored and career-limited. So we contacted a former professor and asked how to become an adjunct faculty member at his alma mater. Now, James works days at the air pollution agency but spends his evenings teaching the next generation of STEM workers in the evenings. His life is so much fuller.

Finally, I once worked with a mechanical engineer named Matt who always wanted to be a DJ. Not a radio station disc jockey, but an utz-utz-utz DJ at a club.

What mid-career professional in his right mind would leave a job with benefits to be a DJ? Nobody, which is why Matt and I worked on two plans: being promoted from a manager to a director of engineering, which pays more and keeps him on a path toward savings and retirement, while also contacting DJs on LinkedIn to ask for career advice. (Yes, LinkedIn!)

Matt still isn't a full-time club DJ—mostly because he's a middle-aged dude with a family and bills to pay—but he's been promoted to director of engineering at his organization. And in his downtime, Matt also has a new group of DJ friends—people who love music and have hobbies and interests outside of work—and has more fun in his life thanks in large part to LinkedIn. That's *truly* something I never thought I'd write!

Taking control of your career, betting on yourself, and putting yourself first can be such innocuous statements—the fluffy stuff of self-help books and motivational seminars. But if you have specific dreams, and know who you are and what kind of risk you're willing to tolerate, these statements provide excellent advice. You don't have to quit your job to find happiness, and there's no need to be paralyzed by fear at work.

Do the premortem, visualize what you want, start small, and get out in the real world to talk with people who are living the life you wish you had. If you're waiting for some asshole at work to give you permission to chase your dreams, you'll always be disappointed. The only person who will ever take a full-throated risk and bet on your success in this crazy world of work is you. And you deserve to flourish.

4

Fix Your Money

YOU CAN'T QUIT YOUR JOB
IF YOU'RE BROKE

People pay money to see others believe in
themselves.

—KIM GORDON

Have you ever looked at your paycheck and thought,
Why am I not rich? You work hard and play by the
rules. Whenever the chance arises, you try to be a good
leader, colleague, and mentor. When it comes time for the
annual review, your contributions are recognized, and you
welcome constructive feedback. So why do you feel inse-
cure about money?

The reason is simple: your job isn't designed to make you
rich. Corporate compensation programs exist to pay you the
least amount of money you'll accept with the promise that,
if you work hard, you might earn more. But performance at

work doesn't equate to financial security. Ever. In fact, it's not uncommon to work your butt off and only wind up with a 3.2 percent annual merit increase to show for your efforts. Contractors and consultants almost never earn more money, either.

The hard truth is that your job exists to make *other* people rich. You're simply the mechanism, not the beneficiary, of all that hard work. You're also not rich because wealthy people keep most of the money. Wage inequality is a pervasive issue that affects women, people of color, members of the LGBTQ+ community, veterans, and disabled workers. But it also affects your cousin who voted for Trump. He has some privilege, but his wife and daughters are underpaid for their work. His family is getting ripped off, too.

I am petty, and one of my favorite things to do is blame people for problems I can't easily solve. We can always point fingers at CEOs and executive leaders. Their pay in America has skyrocketed 940 percent since the 1970s.* Universities and foundations have spent millions of dollars trying to solve the wage gap between workers and executives, but they often ignore one fundamental truth: executives think they deserve it. They run their lives like a business and *always* put themselves first.

I've spent my entire career surrounded by men and women who feel entitled to earn three hundred times more than the average worker. They receive job offers

---

* https://www.epi.org/publication/ceo-compensation-2018/.

and ask for more, get bonuses and wonder why they're not higher, are granted stock options and then ask why the package isn't more lucrative. They are not ashamed to milk every last drop from the corporate cow, and they'll gladly accept an extravagant compensation package while lecturing the average worker on frugality.

Once, early in my career at a company dinner, I drank too much and complained about my seemingly meager salary to a colleague. Nobody likes a whiner, but I spent half my check on the simple act of living: health care, student loans, housing, food, transportation, and buying ugly clothes to wear in the office. I was working to cover the costs of working.

Unfortunately, I was complaining to the chief operating officer, who laughed and said, "You just need to learn how to budget."

Long before baby boomers lectured millennials on skipping avocado toast, they were lecturing Gen Xers on the moral imperative of doing more with less.

That COO thought my life would be different if my parents had taught me how to balance a checkbook. He told me that my generation needed to stop wasting money on unnecessary expenses like mobile phones and entertainment. I would have more money left at the end of the month if I just controlled my spending like the adult I was supposed to be.

I almost went for his throat.

This dude earned over a million bucks a year as his base pay. Beyond that, he qualified for bonuses, restricted stock awards, and a long-term incentive plan, which brought his total cash compensation closer to $2 million.

He got other perks, too.

When he didn't want to move to the town where our headquarters were located, the company subsidized his travel and secondary housing. They gave him an expense account, a company car, concierge health care, executive retreats to beautiful locations where his family could join him, and company-paid tax help because his salary wasn't just a salary—some of his earnings were capital gains—and thus his financial life was complicated.

This old man didn't spend a dime on dry cleaning, gas for his car, or food when he traveled on business, but he felt compelled to lecture me on making a budget.

Sometimes, rich people can't help themselves. They love lecturing the poor and middle class on the morality of money despite their well-known elite tax breaks and shameless salaries.

This is an example of the hypocrisy that drove me out of HR and into freelance consulting in 2008. I became so disillusioned about my time in corporate America that I vowed to work only with socially responsible companies and leaders who cared about employees, communities, and the planet. The list of prospective clients was small, and I had no income for the first six months.

Now, to be fair, most companies don't make a profit in the first year—or ever. Also, launching a small business is far more expensive than I realized. I did not understand how much to allocate for incorporating fees, business cards, website hosting, toner cartridges, my used office chair, or the gas it took to drive to FedEx and fax contracts to clients.

Who the hell uses a fax machine in this century? I'll tell you who: the large corporations and universities you know by name. God forbid they invest in technology. They'd rather keep a fax machine—and more of their profits—than invest in improving their infrastructure and making life easier for employees and vendors.

Each day with my new business was a unique journey into the underreported costs of entrepreneurship. I learned that it's $6/month to have a branded email account, $59 a year for reliable video conferencing, $43 bucks to buy a password manager so I don't get hacked, and $300 a year for accounting software to tell me that I'm not rich. All those expenses were necessary, and I bridged the gap with my American Express platinum credit card with 29.9 percent interest that I had planned to pay off every month.

Even if you have a bunch of clients, revenue doesn't appear in your Bank of America business checking account on day one. I learned quickly that wealthy corporations don't like to part with their money—even when they owe you. You have to chase it. And man, have I.

I've spent six months or longer chasing down checks from companies where CEOs make a thousand times more than their employees, learning that accounts payable departments are full of people who know nothing about the gig economy and do not give a rip if they pay you.

Do you think their CEO waits six months for his money? Heck no.

Not all small businesses have my bad luck with cash flow, but many do. So, after months of trying to solve this problem alone, I asked the most successful person I know for help. His name is Don MacPherson, and he's the former cofounder of a technology company called Modern Survey and the current host of the *12 Geniuses* podcast. Don and his partners sold their Minneapolis-based company to Aon in 2016 for an "undisclosed amount of money." That's a classy way of saying he's rich, by the way, although I think he prefers the word *comfortable*. (And when someone says they're comfortable, they are wealthy.)

Don understood my financial predicament. He grew up in a mining community in northern Minnesota plagued by economic insecurity and unemployment. There, financial illiteracy and reckless spending were the standard ways of living.

In high school, Don saw a random commercial for a financial services company. The actor said if you save $300 a month from the time you're twenty-two until you're thirty, it's like saving $300 each month from the time you're thirty until you retire at sixty-five.

If you're bad at math like me, it's saying: get started early.

The commercial made an impression on Don. His first job out of college was in customer support for American Express, where he earned $17,000 a year. And he began saving $300 each month.

I like to tell myself that I couldn't fix my money in my twenties and think about retirement because of student debt from Sallie Mae. Don had student loans, too, but met his financial commitments and savings goals by skipping the new car, wearing modest clothing, and living in a small apartment. After twenty-four months, Don saved enough money to quit his first job and buy a one-way ticket to Germany where he played professional basketball for a year, while also working part-time in a warehouse and continuing to save up.

When Don returned to America, he kept up with his frugal lifestyle and saving goals. He started Modern Survey with friends and former colleagues from American Express. And the business survived through the Great Recession without layoffs because it had money in the bank to invest when times were lean.

Maybe Don was born with a thrifty gene, but he developed his conservative financial persona by delaying gratification and keeping his eye on the prize: autonomy.

When I asked Don how to dig myself out of a hole and rebuild my business, he offered this life advice:

"You need to pay yourself first."

I wasn't sure what he meant because it felt like I had been paying myself with nice speaker-lady clothes, a new car in the garage, and a whole bunch of debt on my American Express card.

Don went further and explained, "You can only do your best work if you provide yourself with the security and freedom to make good choices. Debt enslaves you. When you are financially secure and free, you never have to compromise or work with clients you don't love. *That's* freedom."

Sounds great, I know. But paying yourself first when you're broke is a challenge. The average American has about $38,000 in personal debt, not including a home mortgage, and over forty million adult Americans carry a student loan, mounting up to nearly $2 trillion in student debt.* It's hard to make financial decisions about the future when the bulk of your paycheck is dedicated to the past. But I took his advice and, through trial and error, learned how to pay myself first.

First, I found a local financial adviser with an expertise in small businesses. We moved my financial statements from Excel and a shoebox to QuickBooks, and we stopped running my company like it was a family pizzeria. Then we set up monthly meetings to review my spending.

The days of my Fortune 500 tastes on a Ruettimann budget ended. Gone were the nights at the Peninsula Hotel or the JW Marriott and a beauty crew to help me look fabulous before speaking engagements. Instead of sleeping in luxury, I booked budget hotels and got my hair blown out at Drybar the night before, then didn't wash my hair for five days. With a little lipstick from Walgreens, I looked almost the same onstage.

---

* https://www.cnbc.com/2018/02/15/heres-how-much-the-average-student -loan-borrower-owes-when-they-graduate.html.

I also took out a low-interest loan to pay off my business credit card debt. A year later, after staying on top of payments, I paid it all back and reconfigured my business and scheduled more pro bono work.

Once my money was fixed-ish, I felt like my business gained speed. Instead of paying compound interest to a faceless bank run by executives who don't know me, I paid myself first by building a cushion for leaner times. Yes, I missed those nights in gorgeous hotels, but I didn't miss the stress of endless credit card payments and high interest rates. With a little room to breathe, I could consult and advise organizations on how to fix work without feeling secretly like an impostor.

You can't fix work—and have reasonable options for your career—unless you fix your money situation first. I'm not one of those leaders who wants to shame you for feeling broke. I don't want you to starve, suffer, or live an austere lifestyle. But paying off your debt and saving for retirement, even slowly and incrementally, is an investment worth more than you can calculate.

DON'T HOLD BACK, YOU FOOL: ASK FOR MORE

The thing I love most about being a professional speaker is talking to women and employee resource groups about social justice issues. I find it incredibly fulfilling to debunk HR myths and offer career advice to historically marginalized communities. But, unfortunately, most of those groups want me to work for free.

"Can you come to Rome and talk to one thousand women about how to succeed in the business world?"

"Are you able to fly to Houston and speak to recent LGBT+ college graduates on how they should navigate the corporate interview process?"

Sure, I would love to, but it's not easy to travel all over the world and stick to my budget.

When these requests first started coming in, I wasn't sure how to handle them. I asked a friend who did a ton of pro bono work, and she said, "Ask for more."

Money isn't the only form of currency. If you can't be paid in cash, try being paid in opportunities that expand your reputation. Develop a meaningful relationship with someone powerful. Get paid in discretionary paid time off (PTO), workplace flexibility, or a chance for a promotion. These are just a few examples of ways to gain "more."

In my case, if an event planner can't cover my speaking fee, I look at my savings account and determine if the opportunity is worth my investment. Then I ask if there's budget for other incidentals: airfare, hotel, food, or car service to the airport. I see if it's possible to meet with the event sponsors and ask if they might advertise on my podcast. I negotiate a high-quality video recording of my session. Sometimes, I score free tickets and bring friends.

My advice is simple: don't be a chump. Ask for more. The worst thing that can happen is they tell you no. And while it feels awkward to be rejected, it feels worse to miss out on more money, opportunity, and access.

Remember, executives ask for more all the time. Salary. Stock options. Bonuses. Additional PTO. Extra personal hours on the company jet. A nanny who travels with you and your baby if business takes you away from home. When you work in human resources, you see firsthand how leaders carry themselves into salary negotiations—with a sense of entitlement. And if you don't gather the courage to ask like they do, you'll never get what they are given.

o o o

The problem with asking for more is that most people do it at the *wrong time*.

For example, let's say you just read an article about asking for a raise. The advice was solid, and you've drawn up a business case to outline the way you've helped your company earn more money. In your pitch deck, you've created a compelling narrative that links your specific actions to increased revenue and greater organizational visibility in the marketplace. You're a rock star, and it's time for your boss to show you the money.

That's a brave request, and I'm super proud of you. Too bad your timing is probably off.

Most companies offer raises and promotions at specific

times of the year. You get reviewed at the end of the year and raises come in January. You talk to your boss in May and then mid-year promotions and raises come around in July or August. Even when you're courageous and finally ask, your off-cycle request won't go anywhere. So, step one, let's fix your money and get that raise by asking at the *right time*.

Here's an overview of how corporate compensation works. There's a season to everything. If your company is publicly traded, the seasons are probably clear and well known. They might be posted on the company's intranet or found in the employee handbook. If compensation cycles aren't clear, you have an HR department. Go talk to them. If you work for a privately held company—or a small-to-medium-size organization—you might have to ask around or befriend the longest-serving administrative professional for the inside scoop. But either way, it's crucial to nail down a compensation cycle because it can take an act of God to push through a regular promotion and raise, let alone an off-cycle merit increase.

When you finally find someone with insight on how people get raises, be ready with questions. Figure out when you should approach your boss for more money or a better title. Discover what language and word choices you should use. Ask about the best supporting evidence to collect and present. And ask yourself, "How could this go wrong?"

When I worked in HR, people would show up in my office out of nowhere and ask for raises on a Tuesday afternoon in the middle of summer at 4:59 p.m.—just as I'm thinking about my long commute home. Who thinks that's a winning strategy to unlock another $15,000 in pay?

I'm not cruel, and I loved listening to workers make a case for a raise. It's inspiring when someone is clear, concise, and confident enough to articulate her reasoning, explain the business case for change, and wait for my response. But I cannot repeat this enough: you need to think like a CEO and make a smart, well-timed argument.

When you ask for a raise out of nowhere, it's called an *off-cycle promotion* or *one-off merit increase*. And those are rarely approved without threat of legal action. How then, you might ask, do you argue for more if the season for raises and promotions is six months or more away?

You don't. You wait.

If you have a lucrative offer and want to leverage it for more money and a better title, you might as well leave for that new job. Sure, you might extort your employer into paying you a little more. You might even get a swanky new job title. But relationships are the currency of business, and people remember how you've made them feel. If you were brazen enough to test the waters and get another job offer that looks better on paper than the job you have, think twice before shoving that new information in your boss's face.

And while I don't have any data to support this, I've found that people who use a competing offer from an outside company to earn more money in their current job end up leaving within six months, anyway.

But this doesn't mean you should give up on asking for more. Once you know your company's compensation cycle, build a business case for change by slowly collecting large and small moments of recognition and storing them in a *brag book*.

The history of the brag book is old. It comes from the pre-Internet days of the late 1980s and early 1990s when smart and talented career coaches like Peggy Klaus* advised candidates to keep a scrapbook of letters of recognition, thank-you notes, and praise from supervisors and peers.

The brag book isn't just for job searches. It's an instrument to help you get a raise or a promotion. If you want something in this world, people need to care about your story. Your brag book serves as a reminder of your hard work, your commitment to the organization, and the multiple ways you've helped the company achieve its goals.

Get on Dropbox or Google Drive and create a virtual folder where you keep positive and affirming text messages, screenshots of social media posts, and even Slack notifications from bosses, customers, clients, and work friends. Turn all of your praiseworthy emails into PDFs and save them. If someone says something positive about you, simply capture it and upload it to the brag book.

Why?

Curating moments of recognition in a brag book becomes helpful during your company's compensation

---

* https://peggyklaus.com/books/.

cycle. These moments can bolster the case for a promotion or merit increase. And, at worst, it just makes you feel good when the odds are against you. Either way, collecting your accomplishments will help you remember your worth, which gives you an emotional and psychological edge during the negotiating process and helps you ask for more. And you deserve it.

WHEN THE MONEY RUNS OUT

Some people blow through their money and are hanging on by a thread.

My father was in this category for most of his life. From as early as I can remember, he had financial problems that interfered with relationships and prevented him from taking a risk and betting on himself.

It didn't start off too badly. My dad was a hippie and a music lover in the early 1970s who found a job at the phone company and kept it for over twenty-five years. It was a blessing for a young man with a high school diploma and no real interest in corporate America. He could show up to work, do his job, and come home without a ton of drama.

My dad wanted something else for his life—something bigger, more audacious—but he couldn't articulate what that was, and thus it was always out of reach. As he got older, the phone company became a mental prison rather than a source of funding for his dreams. He blamed his bosses for his unhappiness and drank J&B scotch whisky to make the days more tolerable.

My father also spent a lot of money to make himself feel better. Some kids grow up listening to Baby Einstein and Barney. I grew up listening to vinyl. My father had an outstanding record collection that included the Who, Pink Floyd, and Blue Öyster Cult. My earliest memory is of flipping through albums that included original recordings from Jethro Tull, King Crimson, and *Chipmunk Punk*—an album where the Chipmunks covered songs like "Call Me" by Blondie, "My Sharona" by the Knack, and "Crazy Little Thing Called Love" by Queen. (It's not real punk, but not bad for a little girl's first exposure to rock music.)

You might not go broke buying records, but you won't grow rich by spending all your cash on impulsive purchases. My father loved going to the movie theater, scoring his kids the most on-trend toys, taking us to amusement parks, and buying scratch-off lottery tickets so my brother and I could join in the fun of winning a few bucks.

Once, my dad won $85 on a lottery ticket and told me it was "found money." What, he asked, should we do with it? Have a nice dinner? Go shopping at the mall? Drive north to an amusement park called Great America and ride the roller coasters?

It's a sweet memory. Found money is fun money. But when I look back at that time, I remember we were renting-to-own a washing machine and receiving collection agency calls about overdue credit card bills. My father spent the lottery money on a three-disc CD player that plugged into his stereo system, even though I don't remember having any CDs. So I'm sure we bought a few of those, too.

There were two moments in my father's life when his financial world came fully crashing down. The first happened when my parents separated in 1982. There is no upside to divorce, and my mother took the family car, leaving my father with a mortgage and a bucket of credit card debt. He asked his parents for help, but my grandparents were not wealthy and couldn't entirely bail him out. My father filed for bankruptcy, which went on to impact his self-esteem and self-worth for decades.

Later in life, the telecom industry imploded and my father accepted a severance package masked as early retirement. Work never made him rich, but the dream of a lump sum cash payout became a nightmare when my dad moved from Chicago to Southern California without a job to reboot his life. He bought a condo he couldn't afford thanks to easy financing right before the Great Recession, and he quickly fell behind with the mortgage payments once his retirement funds ran out.

But that's not to say he didn't try to work.

My father took part in an outplacement program after leaving the phone company, which helps laid-off employees find new employment. Although he refused to go back to school for retraining, he worked with a counselor and applied for just about every position under the sun—qualified or not. And he kept a win-loss spreadsheet to prove that he was making a good-faith effort to find work.

My family did what we could. We gave him money, brought him food, and begged him to stop drinking. My friends in the recruiting industry called him to do "phone screens" and put him in their databases, but they warned me that my father seemed unemployable. He lacked the practical skills to find a corporate job after being out of the workforce for so long.

I was on a business trip to New York City and about to have dinner with a colleague when I learned that my dad was homeless and living in his car. Standing outside the W Hotel in Midtown Manhattan, I googled a Motel 6 from my BlackBerry and booked him a room for a month. Then I offered to pay for rehab, which he declined, though at least he was safe.

After that, my grandmother passed away and left some money to my father. He found a cheap apartment and spent his free time at the public library perusing the Internet. He clicked links, read blogs, and withdrew into himself even more. But while he spent his days online doing nothing, I would argue that he *was* working.

How?

When my dad visited job boards and had his online activity targeted, publishers made money. When he spent time on Facebook looking at old photos and pining for the days when life was easier, tech companies made money. When he searched for temporary gigs that paid cash in a hurry on sites that showed him payday loan ads, ad agencies made money.

It was only my father who didn't reap any of the financial rewards.

My dad was inadvertently working in a new economy where data and attention are currency, yet he was living in the old world where you need a traditional paycheck to survive.

Andrew Yang is a former entrepreneur and 2020 Democratic presidential candidate. He sat down with me in October 2018 and explained how technology companies collect data and profit from online monitoring and surveillance, with no benefit to users.* That's why I believe we should pay people like my father a monthly wage—a basic income or a dividend check for their attention, time, and emotional labor on behalf of brands and technology companies. Instead, we shame them for being addicted to technology while building devices and developing algorithms to hook them more.

But an esoteric argument on the future of work wasn't useful for my dad. As days turned into weeks, and weeks turned into months, my father ran out of options. He never truly saved for the future because as a former phone company employee he never saw himself having one. Ultimately, my father dropped out of the traditional economy and never worked again.

---

* https://laurieruettimann.com/letsfixwork-35/.

Many people would look at my dad as an example of why his original bankruptcy in 1982 was shameful and wasteful. Here's an able-bodied man with a decent job, who always struggled to save more than he spent and never learned from his mistakes. Later in life, he wasn't saddled with emergency medical expenses and had multiple opportunities to make better decisions with his cash. He should've found a job before he moved to California. And when all else failed, he should've tried harder to find temporary work before giving up.

He is a living example of why bankruptcy is wrong.

It's hard to argue with that logic. Except I wonder about who gave him access to credit in the first place. Who sold him a condo he couldn't afford? Who loaned him a cash advance at a 52 percent interest rate for a down payment on his car title knowing full well that he couldn't pay it back? Aren't they partially responsible for this mess?

Now that Donald J. Trump's presidency is a part of our nation's history, we must look at bankruptcy differently. Global financial services companies gave Donald Trump low-interest loans to fund real estate developments and miscellaneous expenditures. His company, the Trump Organization, filed for Chapter 11 bankruptcy four times. Other people took a hit—the banks, contractors, vendors—but Trump never saw a negative impact on the quality of his life.[*]

There are substantial differences between Trump and

---

[*] https://www.nytimes.com/2020/02/04/magazine/deutsche-bank-trump.html.

my father. My dad was born into a working-class family and had bouts of bad luck. There was nobody to bail him out or global banks to write a big check. When he hit rock bottom, there was no help except from family members in the form of temporary housing and loans to tide him over. Bankruptcy was just about the only tool out there that offered him a fresh start. But even that was an imperfect fix because he never did the long-term work to put his emotional well-being first, take control of his career, and become his own agent of change.

Donald J. Trump was born of wealth, worked for his dad, had a network to bail him out whenever he faced a problem, and used his company as a shield to file for bankruptcy four times before he became the forty-fifth president. So is bankruptcy really that bad? Only you can answer that for yourself.

○ ○ ○

Watching what happened to my father informed the principles that I bring to my work. I wish someone had told my dad that if you want a different future, pay yourself first and ask for more in a smart and timely way—not when you're facing homelessness. I also wish someone would have told my father that bankruptcy doesn't have to be shameful. If done right, bankruptcy can reboot your life and give you the chance to go slow, establish a new career identity, and plan for a new version of yourself. Hell, it might even make you the president, one day.

Toni Morrison once told the story of working as a housekeeper for a woman who treated her poorly and didn't pay well. She went home and told her father about her experiences, to which he said: "'Listen. You don't live there. You live here. With your people. Go to work. Get your money. And come on home.'"*

She took it to heart, writing years after she became a household name that work does not—and should not—define who you are as a person. You will have many jobs over the duration of your life, Morrison stressed, but no position or title can ever compare with the value that comes from community.

It might be too late for my poor father, but I know it's not too late for you. Start paying yourself first now.

---

* https://www.newyorker.com/magazine/2017/06/05/the-work-you-do-the-person-you-are.

5

Always Be Learnin'

USE YOUR BRAIN FOR
MORE THAN WORK

When you stop growing you start dying.

—William S. Burroughs

Have you ever had a job where there's nothing to do
and you spend your days surfing the Internet? Or a
job where you want to do more but you are not allowed?

I worked for an insurance company where the CFO
was buying and selling small companies as if he was shop-
ping on Amazon. Even with all that disruption, I didn't
have much to do. Sometimes I'd travel to a satellite office,
say hello, and go sightseeing before flying home. Other
times, I'd drop in on employee meetings and then head
straight to the hotel bar.

When I wasn't on the road, I had an office in down-
town Chicago where I was expected to be available for

HR inquiries and advisory chats with local employees. But nobody ever called. If anything, *I* was the problem child. I would roll into work around 11:30 a.m. and spend my afternoons wandering the city looking at architecture and beautiful churches. Then I took the 4:42 p.m. train home.

One time, I saw Mario Andretti taking photos with fans outside Daley Plaza in Chicago with an Indy 500 race car. I stood in line for an autograph because there was nothing better to do.

"Who's Mario Andretti?" I later asked my husband.

"You need a new job, Laurie."

In many ways, I was the luckiest woman alive. I had total autonomy, lots of responsible people around me who made my life easier, and a strong team of HR generalists who didn't cause trouble. Nobody cared what I did during the day so long as employees weren't suing us, which is refreshing. But I was disengaged and lonely. I'd spend time at the Museum of Contemporary Art in Chicago, then feel guilty about having a job that allowed me to learn about neo-Expressionist paintings but didn't require me to be useful.

The one bright spot in this dull landscape came when a coworker noticed that I was bored and told me about a certification called the SPHR, which is a senior-level designation in human resources offered by the Human Resources Certification Institute.

"Why don't you study for the exam? It's not like you have anything else to do."

To be fair, she was right. I used my corporate Amex

card, bought a binder full of preparation materials, and enrolled in a three-day preparation course at a hotel near O'Hare Airport taught by Mike Losey, the former CEO of an HR association called SHRM.

Mike worked in human resources for over forty years, which seemed insane because I didn't even know HR had been around for that long. There wasn't a single thing Mike didn't know about the world of work, and his passion for HR was contagious.

I took the SPHR exam and passed with flying colors on my first try. When my official test results arrived in the mail, I drove to Hobby Lobby and framed the SPHR certificate. The lady behind the counter talked me into a tacky gold frame with red velour matting because it made me look rich and successful.

I won't pretend that the SPHR certificate solved all my problems. I continued to wander the streets of Chicago and take architectural boat tours to kill time. But those eight weeks of studying for the SPHR changed my life and taught me that I could love the field of HR and human psychology without loving my specific job.

To this day, despite stepping back from the world of corporate HR, I'm still involved in the two biggest HR associations: SHRM and HRCI. And whenever an HR colleague is bored or disaffected, I encourage them to take the SPHR exam or to teach the exam materials—challenging themselves to learn something new and mentor the next generation of HR leaders.

Because chances are, if you hate work, you've stopped learning. Don't just take my word for it. *Harvard Business Review** found employees who are learning at work experience less anxiety and stress, thereby engaging in less unethical behavior than employees on autopilot.

It's not as if studying something different will automatically fix a broken culture or help you oust a corrupt leader who abuses his power. Learning something new is all about *you*. And if you want to take control of your career, you must continue to fix yourself first.

My cousin Beth worked as a receptionist at a busy medical center and hated it. She woke up every morning in a mental fog, threw her hair in a bun, and wore a pair of pale blue medical scrubs even though she wasn't a nurse. When she came home from the office, she complained about her job to anybody who'd listen.

When Beth got the position, I was optimistic. She was, too. At first. She bought new clothes from Ann Taylor Loft, got excited that her office was near a Starbucks, and jumped right into the fray. But her employee experience started to devolve the second she signed the offer letter.

First, there was a toxic culture of envy and mistrust. Every meeting seemed like an episode of *Survivor*. Beth was lost in other people's drama and political agendas. And then there was the fact that job titles and seniority still mattered. Beth's unbridled enthusiasm was suspect.

---

* https://hbr.org/2018/09/to-cope-with-stress-try-learning-something-new.

When her coworkers weren't talking behind her back, they were pulling her aside and telling her to calm down, show some respect, and pay her dues.

"It's nice that you're eager. *But stay in your lane.*"

Have you heard that before? Of course! Few of us go through life without being told to back off. HR managers. Teachers. Lawyers. VPs of sales. Pharmacists. Retail workers. Bakers. Delivery drivers. Landscape designers. Security guards. One person's discretionary effort is another person's threat.

Since people kept telling Beth to back off, she stopped showing up early, staying late, and volunteering to fill gaps in the schedule when her colleagues needed time off. She also quit caring about the patients in her office and her essential job duties.

One day, Beth drove to the store during her lunch hour to buy shampoo and dog toys and to get a break from the office. As she approached the checkout lanes, a group of noisy men stormed the store and began yelling at the cashiers and holding protest signs.

If you remember America's dodgy history with the LGBTQ+ community, you'll recall that in 2016, some people were obsessed with how transgender people went to the bathroom. One retail chain implemented a policy allowing transgender individuals to use the bathroom aligned with their gender identity, causing protests across the United States.

Beth saw the protesters and was overwhelmed with

rage. She screamed back until they left the store. Someone caught the whole exchange on video and posted it to You-Tube. Shortly after, I got the call to intervene.

"Laurie, have a look at the video online. Can you see my face? Will I get fired?"

It was a valid question. Beth had a right to worry. Some American workplaces would fire her in a heartbeat for expressing her point of view while displaying a name tag or badge. It's far more common than you assume and applies to all political protests, from the fight for indigenous land rights to Black Lives Matter. Companies will either make up an excuse related to performance or just dismiss you without explanation.

Thankfully, the video was blurry and it was difficult to recognize her face. All you saw was an exasperated millennial wearing baggy medical scrubs.

But then a funny thing happened in the weeks after our discussion.

Beth rewatched the video and saw herself come alive in the face of intolerance and discrimination. When those protesters pressed forward, she pushed back.

She got curious about herself and wondered why she leaned into the battle when others ran away. Why did she step up and fight when it would've been easier to ignore the protesters and head back to her office?

When you're curious, you are on fire.

Curiosity is a motivational force for high performers. It's a primary driver for learning, personal development, and growth. Experts agree that employees who are inquisitive show more flexibility when solving problems than bored workers.*

Beth expressed more passion in ten minutes at the store than she had in the last ten months at her job, and she wondered if it was possible to find a role that amplified this newly discovered emotion.

That's when she came back to me—finally ready to make a change.

"Can you help me find a job where I can yell at people and get paid for it?"

I wish. That sounds great.

Instead, we searched for positions where Beth could reboot her career, learn something new, and make an impact. We found a veterinarian practice in her area that was hiring receptionists who had an interest in being technicians. It wasn't a perfect match, but animals need as much help as people. If she worked there for three years, they would pay for her schooling and state license.

Beth submitted her résumé and cover letter, interviewed, and was hired within two weeks. She went back to school, studied hard, and invested in continuing education credits. Now, Beth is a licensed vet tech who volunteers in the community, spaying and neutering cats, dogs, potbellied pigs, and just about anything with testicles or ovaries.

My cousin still hates some people, but she enjoys her

---

* https://www.hbs.edu/faculty/Publication%20Files/Let%20your%20workers%20rebel_b87d0da9-de68-45be-a026-22dee862e6e4.pdf.

new career path. When I asked her to reflect on why she was so unhappy at the medical center, her answer was straightforward: she was bored and depressed.

"Maybe not clinically depressed, but my brain was disengaged. It's so much better when you wake up with a purpose and challenge yourself to learn something new."

By changing jobs, Beth didn't just learn a new skill. She took a risk on herself, learned how to be helpful, and used her knowledge to do more than earn a paycheck—she's reducing the unwanted pet population in her community. She stopped thinking the cure for monotony and unhappiness was to blame other people. Instead, she discovered that the solution to career boredom is learning something new.

Career breakthroughs come in many forms, but they all start with learning. Maybe you're stuck in a job that eats your soul alive, or maybe your business is too small to promote you to the next iteration of your career. It makes sense to look for a new role, but try learning something new before you say goodbye to that existing paycheck. You might be surprised.

My friend Samantha is a former sales and marketing professional who took eleven years off to raise a family. Returning to work isn't easy for most mothers, but Samantha's challenge proved more difficult than most: during her time as a stay-at-home mom, she developed a love of Pilates, went back to school, and achieved a senior-level designation. While her kids were young, Samantha spent time tutoring private clients on how to strengthen their core and stand up straight.

Unfortunately, Pilates pays poorly. Wealthy women will spend upward of $100 for a private lesson, but instructors earn less than a third of that. They are independent contractors and don't earn health or retirement benefits in America. If you're lucky, you work for a studio that pays you in culture with a flexible schedule and nice people who encourage learning and growth. If you're like most instructors, you bounce around.

Samantha loved Pilates, but she loved paying her mortgage and taking her kids on vacation more. And she didn't enjoy working for studio owners who treated her like an employee—with all the criticism, feedback, and demands for her time and energy—yet didn't offer the accompanying benefits. Bored with the never-ending pursuit of a perfect job, she took fate into her own hands and learned how to run a business.

Samantha enrolled in a sped-up MBA program while raising her children and continuing to teach Pilates on the side. During the graduate program, she felt so guilty for being away from the family that she agreed to do anything to make her kids happier. Like smart children, they asked for a puppy and Samantha agreed, knowing full well that taking care of an animal would fall on her. (Which it did.) But nevertheless, she pushed through and graduated at the top of her class.

Those plans to open a Pilates studio and control her

own destiny were great, but they never happened. Instead, Samantha got a sales internship at a sports marketing agency and truly enjoyed the experience. After graduation, the firm offered her a full-time job.

Samantha was temporarily stuck, but she wasn't helpless. When I asked her why she pursued an MBA after all those years, she told me that one of her students went through a graduate program while working and inspired her to try the same.

"I had to see it work for someone else before I could claim it for myself."

I asked Samantha about the challenges of working and raising a family while learning something new. She said that the only point when she thought about quitting school was when they initially rescued the puppy.

"She was harder to manage than my accounting class. We'd give her a bath, put her down on the ground, and she would run and pee at the same moment. I won't lie. I sat on my kitchen floor and cried."

But the new job that uses Samantha's brain is great. She said, "I'm never bored at work. All that hard work in graduate school was worth it."

Not everyone needs an MBA, but everybody needs to learn. Whenever I have a troubled client asking for career advice, we focus on first learning something new in the next thirty days. Whether it's an exhausted CEO or an antisocial customer service representative stuck in a corporate job, we don't take self-assessments or pay a consultant to administer the MBTI, a personality test, in order to learn more about ourselves. We look to the data that already exists and figure out our learning journey. You can do this, too.

Grab a cup of coffee, go somewhere quiet, and reread your most recent performance review. Or think about the last time someone gave you constructive feedback that rubbed you the wrong way. What did they say, and why did it bother you? What did they want you to do differently?

Even if you disagree with the data, try to fix it.

Hit the Internet. Google it. There is no problem you're facing at work that someone else hasn't solved. Look for a course you can take or a specific skill you can practice to address the feedback you got.

Keep a journal and document what you're learning for the next thirty days. Here are some examples.

"Today I started a 'finance for nonfinancial professionals' class and it was hard."

"Here are the three things I learned from my LinkedIn Learning course on managing workplace conflict."

"I just fumbled my way through a Toastmasters meeting, but I now know that it's a safe space for failure."

If you need accountability, email hello@letsfixwork .com and we can work on this together. At the end of your thirty-day journey, write out five things you've learned about yourself and five things that surprised you about the past month. Send them to me. I promise you'll have exceeded the expectations of your last performance review.

And if you don't have a recent performance review, ask a colleague for help. Schedule an informal meeting, grab lunch, or take a walk around the building. Ask these two questions:

"What's one specific behavior I can learn in the next thirty days to improve our relationship? Or can you give me an example of a behavior that hinders better communication between us?"

Then shut up and listen.

Even if you don't agree with what you hear, stifle the impulse to defend yourself and explain your actions. Thank your coworker for being candid. Then meet with your buddy again in thirty days and discuss your progress. Look for solutions online as outlined in the exercise above.

The behavior your coworker mentions? The one you need to fix? It will be the thing everybody in your office has been dying to tell you about.

Maybe you talk too much in meetings, your attendance is unsatisfactory, or your coworkers think you are messy. Maybe you're not meeting a sales quota because your communication skills are insufficient and it's dragging down the team. Maybe your boss thinks you are surrendering too soon and not trying to solve customer problems before escalating issues up the chain of command.

Whatever the feedback, you are strong enough to accept and address it. At the very least, you can try. All they're asking you to do is learn from past mistakes and grow.

MENTORS MAKE THE ULTIMATE DIFFERENCE

The Internet loves life hacks. Want to remove grass stains? Use soda water. Need to make a tasty grilled-cheese sandwich? Use mayo, not butter. (It sounds gross, but it's delicious!)

Unfortunately, there are no life hacks for learning at work. As much as you want to know the top three things to say to your boss for a raise—or the seven ways to close a deal with reluctant prospects—the workplace doesn't operate that way. Human behavior is much more nuanced than articles on the Internet make it seem, and there's too much variability in our personalities for these hacks to be effective.

But if you're looking for the next closest thing: get a mentor.

Late in my HR career, I provided support to a group of IT professionals in our St. Louis office. It wasn't a glamorous job, but it was nice to talk to people who still had jobs, and I tried to be available for employee-related emergencies and advice.

One afternoon, the local office manager called me in distress and asked me to open my email in-box that very moment. It was a level-six personnel emergency, but he didn't have time to explain the working definition of *personnel* or *level six*.

I logged on to my laptop and read a forwarded email from a manager named Bella. While venting to a colleague in her department, she referred to her VP of IT as an assbag.

You read that right—an assbag.

Bella was in a meeting where her boss was being a jerk. In a moment of frustration, she emailed a colleague and expressed her annoyance. Instead of coaching Bella to communicate with respect, the coworker stabbed her in the back and forwarded her email to several people in the office including the office manager and the VP.

You can imagine what happened next. People pretended to be appalled, the VP was offended, and the pitchforks were out. A level-six assbag crisis was born.

The office manager wanted to know if I could hop on a plane to St. Louis and fire Bella. He asked if I could be there by 7:00 a.m. the next day and perp-walk her out of the building before anybody else heard about it.

I replied, "Hey, can we just show up at her house and throw a rock through her window? Can we knock on her window and startle her in the Dunkin' Donuts drive-thru before she begins her daily commute?"

He didn't think it was funny.

I told the office manager that I would fly down and fire Bella, but first he'd have to answer some HR questions for me. How much would it cost to defend the organization from a lawsuit? How much time and energy will we spend managing the gossip and intrigue? And how will other women react when they learn that Bella was ambushed in a parking lot and fired for expressing herself?

The office manager agreed we shouldn't fire Bella on the spot, but I didn't trust him not to cause additional drama. So I flew down to St. Louis and met with the leadership team and the VP of IT to defuse the situation. I also pulled Bella into a conference room and asked her, "Assbag? What the hell were you thinking?"

I'm a classy HR leader like that.

Bella couldn't muster the energy to respond and cried for five straight minutes. She accidentally snot-sobbed onto my Petite Sophisticate blazer and Talbots blouse, ruining it. (Dang, I loved that outfit. I felt so grown-up while wearing it.)

Bella had the potential to be a fabulous manager, but the politics of her job frustrated her. It's painful to be gossiped about by coworkers and office managers, but sometimes people have to learn lessons about restraint the hard way—by making mistakes and getting called out.

Bella had a few options. She could continue to play the victim and get angry with corporate policies and heartless leaders. Or she could follow my advice and mimic great leaders to rebuild her reputation, taking ownership of her career and learning from this mistake.

Once she stopped crying, she chose the latter and said, "I'd like the opportunity to fix this mess."

We made a plan to move forward based on three principles that will save just about anybody's ass at work: *accountability*, *contrition*, and *action*.

Accountability means you take ownership of whatever

problem you caused with professionalism and integrity. It was your responsibility to get it right, but you made a mistake and screwed up. You blew it.

Contrition is a two-part process. It's an expression of a remorseful statement that shows you understand how your behaviors impacted others. But it's also a commitment to change. Yes, you were wrong. Now vow to fix it.

Action is what you do after you've made a mistake. It's how you make good and demonstrate that you're sorry. Choose two or three key things you'll do differently so this never happens again, and do them.

Accountability, contrition, and action. That's what it takes to get a second chance.

Later that morning, Bella stood at the head of the table in a taupe-on-taupe conference room and apologized for being disrespectful and immature. She promised to learn from her mistakes and prove she deserved her management role. And she agreed to work with HR and improve her communication skills, her leadership style, and how she expresses anger.

When she sat down, I told the team it's tough to be a young woman with a lot of potential who has never had to navigate the complexities of a large corporation before. Weren't we all a version of Bella when we started out— eager, anxious, and passionate?

I'm sure people rolled their eyes, but I promised to find a successful leader at the company who could mentor

Bella. The plan was basic: they would meet and talk about obstacles, challenges, and corporate politics. At the end of ninety days, we'd reconvene and have an honest discussion about Bella's performance.

Everybody agreed to move forward. And I introduced Bella to Nancy—her new mentor.

What I loved about Nancy was that she had over twenty years of experience but still kept her sense of hope and optimism. Even when men treated her like a secretary instead of an IT leader, she showed no signs of anger.

When I requested Nancy's help, she had only one question.

"What's an assbag?"

To this day, I still don't know. It might be a general term for someone who sucks. Might be a colostomy bag. Or it might be a hemorrhoid pillow people use on long airplane trips. I never asked Bella to explain the origins of the word.

Once Nancy began mentoring Bella, I saw an immediate improvement in performance and morale. Bella was less abrasive and seemed genuinely excited to have a workplace ally. Her colleagues backed off. Nobody called me with level-six personnel emergencies.

All credit to Bella (and Nancy). She got the message, worked hard, embraced the opportunity to start fresh, and enrolled in leadership courses at the Center for Creative Leadership (CCL). Bella learned how to communicate with maturity and compassion in a high-pressure environment, and she worked hard to earn back the trust of her team.

After the ninety-day probationary period, Bella and I reviewed her progress. She was happier and thanked me for being in her corner as she learned how to better navigate corporate America.

"I'm surprised I didn't get fired."

To be honest, me too. I still can't believe we pulled it off.

Bella came to her role with specialized skills and an abundance of technical expertise. But, as famous motivational speaker Marshall Goldsmith says, what got you here won't get you there. Sometimes being good at your job isn't enough, and Bella had to admit that her career was broken in order to fix it. She had to learn something new—how to communicate her feelings with *clarity* and *integrity*. And within twenty-four months of the level-six assbag emergency, the leadership team promoted Bella to a senior manager and identified her as a high performer with potential.

Bella didn't waste her one and only opportunity to work with a mentor. She knew she was lucky to get one. More and more men report how uncomfortable they are mentoring women,* and many high-profile executives follow the Billy Graham rule—a practice popular among Evangelical Christians like Mike Pence where they avoid spending time alone with women to whom they are not married. There is

---

* https://www.weforum.org/agenda/2019/05/the-number-of-men-who-are -uncomfortable-mentoring-women-is-growing/.

only one of two reasons why these men won't spend time with women: they are worried about either being aroused or being falsely accused of some heinous act.

One way to fix this issue in the workplace is to fire male leaders who won't spend time with or mentor women. You don't get to cherry-pick specific aspects of your job, so why are you able to opt out of mentoring the next generation of leaders? If you're a man who worries about his reputation at the expense of organizational development, you are not up for the complexities of being a leader. It's time for you to go.

o o o

Before you're called into a conference room by your HR manager, examine the gaps in your career, character, and attitude. Then find someone to help. Mentors don't have to be in your immediate orbit. You can start by mimicking successful people at large. Do what they do. They don't even have to know you're copying them. Go on LinkedIn, search for someone who is living their best life, and watch them online. Read what they've written. Subscribe to their YouTube channel.

I once saw a one-minute video of Suzy Welch on Twitter. Suzy is a famous American businesswoman and the wife of Jack Welch, the former CEO of General Electric. Suzy talked about the 10-10-10 rule for making tough decisions. Here's how it works. You ask yourself how a situation and outcome will feel in ten minutes, ten months, and ten years. Spoiler alert: you'll make better decisions for the future if you focus on the ten-year goal.

That video clip spoke to me. Since then, I found out it might be the Warren Buffett rule for decision making. I don't care. I'm now a Suzy Welch acolyte. She's my mentor. She doesn't know me, but she changed my life.

And that's what makes mentorship the single biggest hack for fixing work. Bella had Nancy to help overcome the level-six assbag crisis. I have Suzy Welch. Who do you have?

FEEDBACK CUTS DEEP

I must pause for a moment and admit that adaptation and growth are the challenges of a lifetime—even for someone like me who remains committed to self-improvement.

Sometimes I'm tired. Sometimes I'm lazy. Even when I know my blind spots, I don't want to try until I'm pushed.

A colleague named Cameron once told me, "Laurie, you eat like a wild dog."

He wasn't wrong.

We were at a fancy restaurant in the neighborhood next to the United Nations headquarters in New York City, celebrating a colleague's retirement, and Cameron noticed that I scarfed down my food like an orphan in a novel by Charles Dickens.

All night, Cameron watched me fumble with my fork and use my hands as utensils. At one point, he caught me dipping my bread into a swath of butter and steak juice smeared on my plate. Then, to make things worse, I licked my fingers.

He might've puked in his mouth.

To be fair, Cameron was a snob who spent his whole life in a fancy neighborhood in New York City. I was raised for a period of time by my grandmother, who cooked assembly-line-style for eight grandkids. Our diet was mostly soft foods like oatmeal, spaghetti, and chicken nuggets, and we used sporks—those spoon and fork combos given out at fast-food restaurants—to minimize the dirty dishes. When something like meat loaf needed to be sliced, Gramma took care of it.

After Cameron's comment, I pushed my plate away and declined dessert. I felt ashamed. It was humiliating to be called out in public.

The next day, Cameron apologized, but he still had questions about my table manners.

"How did you get this far eating like that?"

Leave it to a New Yorker to ask a direct question.

I told Cameron about my grandmother's food preparation strategy. With all those kids, there was no time for formal etiquette lessons. The result? I ate like Oliver Twist.

"Didn't someone try to teach you manners?"

Sure, my high school boyfriend tried to intervene and teach me how to use a knife, but I was a slow learner. It was easier to eat simple foods like soup, sandwiches, and pizza than learn something new.

"I'm sorry to hear about your weird childhood," Cameron said, "but there's this thing called YouTube. Maybe watch a video on etiquette. You can't eat pizza forever."

Couldn't I?

Listen, it's not like I didn't know that my table manners were atrocious. What caught me off guard was that someone saw me in my raw element—immature, undignified, making a lazy choice to stay in the past—and said something.

We each have blind spots and skill deficiencies. But I'm here to tell you that the time to learn from your mistakes and fix those blind spots is now. Other people see the behaviors and problems you're ignoring, and they feel sorry for you even if they express it poorly. Who knows, your idiosyncrasies might even be career-limiting.

Since that day when Cameron called out my table manners, I've watched YouTube videos and sat through corporate etiquette lessons from friends and consultants. I've also read *Emily Post's Etiquette* and blogged about my journey with table manners at fine-dining restaurants. I won't be having tea with the queen of England soon, but, if it happens, I'm ready.

It took an embarrassing moment in public, and a bit of manners shaming, to coax me into taking control of my life. So I wonder: What's your point of weakness, and what will it take for you to fix it?

Maybe you're a whistler, a heavy breather, or someone who hums a tune at his workstation while others are making calls. Or maybe you crack your knuckles during meetings, always forget your wallet, and don't know how to read a map.

Stop ignoring your flaws and choosing the easy way in life. There will be a moment in your career when it's too late to fix the issue.

My friend John ran an underperforming sales department that failed to meet expectations. There weren't enough outbound calls. Inbound inquiries sat in a queue. And the employees never seemed to worry about quotas until the end of the quarter.

"It's all marketing's fault," John told anybody who listened. "We need better enablement tools."

What's an enablement tool? Don't worry about it. It's corporate-speak—something that somebody says when they're too lazy to take ownership of a problem. It's easier to blame others for shortcomings than to consider our role in the mess we've created. If I had to guess, John had been making excuses like this his whole life.

It should come as no surprise that John's boss André was furious with the output of the sales team. You can't really call it "sales" if nobody is closing deals, so André scheduled a hackathon to generate new ideas on how to transform the team and improve the sales funnel.

And he did this without John's input.

A hackathon is an event where many people meet over several days to engage in collaborative computer programming. In today's modern world of work, the principles are now applied to problem solving across multiple departments. John's boss invited anybody in the organization who cared about sales to meet in the company kitchen and brainstorm creative ways to increase sales.

John's misplaced confidence in his outdated skills, combined with his laissez-faire management style, were no longer effective for the organization. André hired me to be John's executive coach and give him two options: leave with a severance package or embrace this teachable moment to become the leader he was meant to be.

That's how it goes for executives, by the way. Nobody ever gets fired. We pay for them to go.

"We don't need a hackathon to fix my sales team," John insisted. "André is a jerk. And what does somebody in procurement or graphic design know about closing a deal? This is my team. We'll work through this."

Sometimes coaching is about listening, and sometimes it's about speaking truth to power. I said, "John, they're not your sales team. You don't pay their salaries. They report to you on an organization chart at a company where you work at the pleasure of the CEO. Right now, André is not happy. Your days are numbered."

Now I'd gotten his attention and said, "I don't work in sales. But I use a tool called the premortem to predict how I will fail. What if your sales reps recorded all the ways they'd fail before an important meeting with a prospect? If they worked backward and could see how the meeting will go bad, they'd be ready for anything."

John thought it over and told me that it was a great idea.

"Welcome to a hackathon, my friend," I said. "It's a bunch of people sitting around, thinking of ideas, and trying to move the needle forward like I just did. Not every idea will be terrific, but there's nothing to fear. Now keep your job and go learn something from your coworkers who care about sales."

No matter who we are, continuous learning is a challenge. But we can each change our lives if we attempt to learn a little more today than we did yesterday.

Beth didn't realize she had the potential to find a job she enjoyed and be a fighter for the underdog. Bella didn't know how to channel her frustration and transform into a leader. John didn't grasp how to run a twenty-first-century sales team. And I didn't learn how to use a knife until somebody's feedback cut me deep. The solution for almost every obstacle in your career is to double down on learning. As long as there's an opportunity to master new ideas and skills, there's hope. And sometimes hope is all you need to finally take control of your career.

6

Be Your Own HR

HAVE YOUR OWN BACK AT THE OFFICE

> I hope that when machines finally take over,
> they won't build men that break down, as
> soon as they're paid for.
>
> —BOB KAUFMAN

The worst day of my HR career came pretty early on. It was a dark August afternoon. My office was on the third floor of a 1960s-style building with a center courtyard, so I had a view of other offices and the sky. A lightning bolt flashed, and I jumped out of my seat, looking out the window and across the courtyard. That's when I saw a vice president kissing his administrative assistant. The blinds were open. They didn't realize that mirrored windows aren't reflective on a cloudy day.

It took me a second to realize what I was witnessing.

She was seated on his desk, and he had his arms wrapped around her body. It wasn't even that suggestive until he went down on his knees. I screamed, "Oh my god."

My manager sat nearby and usually ignored me. But this time, she looked up from her desk, craned her neck, and glimpsed the scene. What's worse is that I looked out the window and scanned the courtyard of the building. My boss and I weren't the only ones watching. Nearly everybody on the third floor was pressed against the windows. They had all stopped what they were doing to watch the show. Before I could ask what to do, a colleague named Dougie ran over to my desk area and said, "Just want to give you a heads-up. Look out the window. Frank is in his office—killing his career." No shit, Dougie. Thanks for the update.

Nobody did anything to stop the train wreck unfolding in front of us. I stared at my boss. She stared at me. Then I yelled, "Fine, I'll go." I ran halfway around the building like Usain Bolt and knocked on Frank's door. The assistant cracked it open and asked, "Hi, Laurie, what's up?"

I said, "Shut the blinds. We can see."

I thought the poor lady might pass out. She thanked me and closed the door. Seconds later, I could hear them pull the cord to shut the vertical blinds—but it was too late.

Almost immediately, I could feel my heart pounding in my ears. My head hurt and my hands were shaky. Though nothing was wrong with me, I just wanted to break down and call my mom. But I couldn't cry because I had to get back to work—screening résumés and interviewing candidates on the phone. When I wrapped up my calls, I tried to talk to my boss about next steps.

"What's next?" I asked.

She told me nothing was next and added, "It is above our pay grade."

On that day, I learned everything about work and humanity, starting with the fact that people are having sex at work—a lot. You're answering phone calls and attending meetings, but someone is having sex in an office near you. It's gross. Wash your hands at work often.

Also, I learned that people are weasels and find your mistakes entertaining. Sometimes, your coworkers would rather watch you burn your career down in glorious fashion than stick their necks out and help.

And even in HR, leaders are often cowards. When it's time to be accountable, they will assign responsibility to someone higher up the chain of command. Talk to someone powerful about his inappropriate behavior? No thanks, I'd prefer to stare at my computer screen and do some fake-work on the Internet.

Toward the end of the worst day in my career, I went to the cafeteria in search of something to eat. I grabbed a bag of Famous Amos cookies from the vending machine, sat down in the corner by myself, and wiped the tears away from my eyes.

This is of course when Frank's administrative assistant

appeared. She made a beeline for my table, thanked me profusely, and asked, "Do you think a lot of people saw?"

Talk about denial.

I took a deep breath and lied. Nope, I said, I don't think many people watched. It was just my boss and me.

"Good. I don't want Frank to get in trouble."

I was shocked. I thought, you don't want Frank to get in trouble? Is that a joke? And why isn't Frank over here apologizing to me?

I told the assistant that Frank would be fine, but I worried about her future. People talk, and, if history has shown us anything, it's that women never fare well in relationships at work. Frank was under no obligation to shield her from trouble. In fact, I anticipated that he would do the opposite and throw her under a bus.

"We love one another," she said. "He'll take care of me."

I shook my head. Even though I was still new to the world of work, I'd already grasped one important thing: only you take care of you.

Bosses come and go, and HR teams are almost always terrible. The only person you can trust at work is yourself. Don't put your fate in the hands of someone who has financial control over you. Take an active and involved role in your own outcomes and experiences.

The administrative assistant was at least twice my age, and part of me wondered how she made decisions in other areas of her life. I'm sure she doesn't trust the grocery clerk to ring up her items with no mistakes—she scans the receipt. I'm also sure she doesn't believe that the department store removes the anti-theft device from her clothes before she leaves. She looks, just like the rest of us.

Work is like any other transaction: you should trust but verify.

I couldn't help but press further, asking, "Why do you presume that Frank would protect you? Aren't you worried about getting caught having sex at work with your boss?"

She looked at me like I was a naive child and said, "I'd only be worried if you told HR."

I'm like—I *am* HR.

"You know what I mean. You're just a recruiter. And you're cool."

Oh boy. She got that wrong. I got up to buy a second bag of Famous Amos and processed the conversation. Even if I wanted to report this incident, where would I go? Was it okay to turn on my boss and speak to the higher-ups at work? I had no clue, so I bought a third bag and ate them on the commute home.

Those cookies are addictive.

In the end, I listened to my boss over my own instincts and remained quiet. Eventually, when there was a management restructuring, Frank's team merged with another group and his assistant was laid off. He moved to another part of the company. Maybe my boss was right. Maybe it was being handled at a pay grade above ours. But, had I intervened and said something, perhaps that administrative assistant would have kept her job.

Within a year of this bizarre incident, I was also gone. My mom became sick from an illness called hemorrhagic pancreatitis. I didn't have much PTO accumulated, so I took some unpaid but protected time off thanks to Bill Clinton and the Family Medical Leave Act (FMLA). I cared for my younger siblings, who were still in middle school, while ensuring that my mother received the best medical care possible.

While I was out on leave, my boss restructured our department, trying to terminate my position. It was only through government legislation that my job was protected. Eventually, I came back from caring for my mother and stuck around a few months out of spite. Now I look back and am like, *Wow, Laurie, you were so dumb. You should've seen that coming and asked for a severance package.*

I'm here to tell you what I wish I'd known then: you fix work by making one brave choice, then another, and then another, until you see improvements in your daily life. Work is fixed when you put yourself first, take control of your career, and act like your own HR department. Because God knows your local HR team can't always be trusted to do the right thing. (See above.)

Look at the landscape of your life and define the metrics that matter to you. Make career decisions based on the way work aligns with your values. Elevate your physical well-being and emotional health. Prioritize the strength

of your relationships. Don't compromise on your principles. If something feels wrong, try to understand why that
is. Stop dismissing the chaos in your life by explaining it
away as a phase or temporary condition that will improve
when something else changes. And *please* stop waiting for
someone else to fix whatever is wrong.

If we wait for other people to do right by us, we get
Frank—a man who thought nothing of having a relationship with someone he supervised. We also get my manager, an individual unmoved by a blatant abuse of power.
If we continue to wait for leaders and corporations to put
employees first, we'll be here forever.

It's time to stop waiting. If we believe that work can
be a place where people develop their skills and discover
dignity and respect, we need to be the change we wish to
see in the world. When we see injustice and exploitation,
we need to deal with it. When we experience it ourselves,
we must fight back and stop it.

How do you take control of your career when someone abuses power and mistreats you? How can you be
your own HR when systems and policies fail you?

As I've covered in this book so far, there are multiple avenues to personal and professional reclamation. Get
physically and emotionally healthy. Pull yourself out of
isolation and talk to someone—a colleague, a mentor, a
therapist, or an employee assistance provider. Learn to
bet on yourself. It's hard to take risks, but the premortem
is the most effective tool in your arsenal to predict and

beat failure. Ask yourself how something will fail. Write it down. And craft a plan to overcome failure.

It sucks that it's on you—and me, and everybody else—to fix work. But this book is a tool in your arsenal to put yourself first, take control of your career, and be your own HR department. Now go and do it.

WHAT THE F**K DOES HR ACTUALLY DO?

The one thing I inherited from my mom is an open face. It's a condition where everybody thinks you're friendly and wants to tell you their life story—but if you're like me, often you're not that interested and you don't really care. Yet people confess to you anyway, like a priest in a church, and you're helpless to stop it.

This phenomenon of random people talking to me has grown so bad that I've taken to wearing my noise-canceling headphones everywhere, including airplanes, restaurants, subways, and hotel bars when I'm trying to eat dinner. But it doesn't matter. People still approach me regardless.

The last time someone struck up a conversation with me on an airplane, it was an executive from a midsize company who, indeed, told me his life story. But then, after about half an hour, he asked about my job.

"What do you do for a living?"

Keeping it simple, I said, "I'm an HR consultant."

"Ah," he replied. "I've always wondered—why does HR suck? No offense."

Whenever someone tells you not to be offended, prepare to be offended. Especially if the comment comes from a guy in first class.

But I understand why my seatmate thought HR sucks. It often starts at the beginning of the employment process, when someone like you applies for a job and then waits forever to hear back—if at all. Companies regularly interview hundreds of candidates, only to leave the job open indefinitely because they can't find someone who is a good *cultural fit* (whatever that means).

Once hired, the first week will probably look like *Lord of the Flies*. A receptionist shows you where to sit on the first day, someone from IT hands you a laptop (without correct log-on information), and your new-hire paperwork is completed via an anonymous portal. If the company is ahead of the game, a real human will take you on a tour of the cafeteria and show you the closest bathroom to your desk. But that's by no means a guarantee.

If there's an employee orientation, it's not about you. The HR manager makes that very clear. If you're curious about what it really takes to succeed at this company, you're on your own. Instead of having access to an adviser or coach, you get a boring lecture or video that covers all the things you're not supposed to engage in on the job but are probably happening anyway (which is why you're sitting through mandatory training). It doesn't get much better once you're over the hump of being new. If you make it past a year, you are lucky to get a raise and feedback on your performance. But have a problem? Don't bother going to HR because, to be honest, staff there can't be trusted with confidential information at most companies.

Sometimes, your job runs its course and the only reasonable decision is to quit. When you finally find that new job and leave, your manager explains that you're dead to him. Don't let the door hit you on the way out.

HR *could* fix all of this. Instead, it's a mess in most organizations. But it doesn't have to be that way.

I dream of a world where local HR departments prioritize the human beings they were meant to serve. We need human resources teams to stand firm against bullying, harassment, racism, sexism, homophobia, transphobia, misogyny, ableism, xenophobia, and even religious discrimination. HR could do that and much more. It should hire people based on rigorously defined criteria—not based on nepotism or cognitive biases—and then pay them a fair wage. It's on HR to ensure that workers are onboarded with care, equipped to do their jobs. And when it comes time for an employee's annual review, HR needs to step up and guarantee the process remains orderly and transparent.

I'm told some HR teams are doing this already. You may know someone who works in human resources and does a great job. I won't dispute that; however, I think it's far too rare.

But—and here's the kicker—you can't blame an

institution for the reasons why work, specifically *your* work, is broken. In order to make a change, you must be your own HR and your own advocate, at three crucial points in the evolution of your working life: when you're looking for work, when you're joining a company, and when you decide to leave.

HOW TO LOOK FOR WORK LIKE A PRO

Forgive me for stating the obvious, but looking for work is messed up. Most job descriptions are nothing more than marketing tools meant to sell you on a role that doesn't really exist. When you interview, the process is about as reliable as throwing darts at a dartboard while blindfolded. And just because you interview doesn't mean you'll hear back, either. Nobody at your future company cares if the interview process is emotionally taxing. If anything, it's okay if you're unhappy—that's part of corporate hazing.

Searching for a new job is one of the most exhausting and stressful things you can do in life, and that's because it's more than just showing up to sell someone on your skills. You are required to seem interesting and compelling while outsmarting recruiters, hiring managers, and anyone else who thinks they're one step ahead of you. You're asked to carve out time from your schedule and lie to your coworkers about where you're going at two o'clock in the afternoon. And as you're actively lying to your current employer, you must act like a professional and pretend that you'd never lie to your future employer.

The honest truth is that future employers can sense your exhaustion and stress, but they don't care. If your energy is wrong, they'll skip right past your résumé and move on to the next person who shows the appropriate amount of vitality and passion.

This may sound simple and reductive, but trust me. When on the hunt for a new job, mind-set is everything. If you're looking, go back to the single most important lesson of this book: Put. Yourself. First.

Nobody is asking you to join CrossFit—or book a trip to Tijuana for bariatric surgery—but you'll need to build up your endurance in order to stay motivated and empowered when times are tough. And looking for a new job is *always* tough. The same good self-care rules apply: get plenty of sleep, eat foods that nourish you, and kick toxic people out of your life who don't buy into the future that you want.

Next, let's break out the premortem from earlier and apply it to your job search. Think about the last time you looked for work. Reflect on the experience and ask: How did you mess up? What regrets do you have? And how will you blow it this time?

There are universal acts of failure in every job search. Normally, you apply for hundreds of jobs online—even ones that don't make sense—hoping that an applicant tracking system (ATS) will find magical keywords and select your résumé for a phone screen with a recruiter. Or you'll network with other unemployed people instead of thinking about the three to five people who might actually be helpful to you in a job search. Or you talk to your fellow cynical colleagues all day long instead of finding and befriending three to five new people on LinkedIn who currently have your dream job. (By the way, all you have to do is hit that person up on LinkedIn's InMail feature and say, "I saw your profile. You have my dream job. Can I talk to you for fifteen minutes about how you found it?")

The most effective way to find a job might be the least obvious. My friend Ryan Paugh wrote a fabulous book called *Superconnector: Stop Networking and Start Building Business Relationships That Matter.* He told me that the single best way to network with people is to be helpful and of service. If you are known as a sounding board for people in your community, and you have mentored someone, you are in good stead. Being service oriented enables people to think of you as helpful instead of the person who's stuck in a crappy job—or unemployed. Volunteering your time makes you more interesting and likable, and it introduces you to new people who may be helpful in surprising ways. When you help others, you gain their trust, which makes them more likely to offer favors and advice that can benefit you down the road.

Job searches don't have to be dreadful ordeals if you follow my tips. And if you'll notice, it doesn't have anything to do with HR. So stop blaming human resources when you can't find work and go grab the job you deserve.

ONBOARD YOURSELF LIKE A BOSS

The first few days of a new job are awkward and terrible for many individuals, but not for everybody—and not always. Think about the best job you've ever had (if you had one). Chances are your first ninety days were fun and challenging. You laughed a lot, got to know people, and made a bunch of friends. Your goals were clear, the company was supportive, and you spent those days taking care of business without thinking about politics, infighting, or drama.

Based on my experiences, you don't need more than three months to determine if a job is a good fit. You know the first time someone asks you to do something you aren't normally inclined to do: Can you work late? Would you mind making a few extra calls? Can we talk about things that are bothering me?

If you say yes, enthusiastically, to extra emotional and professional work in the early days, the job is a fit. If you hesitate, it's an important indication that something is wrong. That's why the best HR departments will work with you right away to help you feel connected to your team and invested in the organization's goals on an emotional level. If you love the people around you and trust them, you're locked into those relationships and will gladly demonstrate discretionary effort.

Unfortunately, far too many of us don't have access to great leaders who understand the importance of interpersonal connection. It's up to you ultimately to invest in relationships during the first ninety days. So do it. Take an early and active part in your own onboarding. Hit the ground running by asking questions before you even start.

How can I get to know my colleagues before day one? What's the best way to learn about cultural norms? Can I connect with IT ahead of time, so my new laptop and phone are ready to go? Is it okay if I connect with my team before day one?

Bottom line: make important connections with people as fast as you can. Find your manager on LinkedIn and scan her first- and second-degree relationships before the first day. Try to find your new coworkers and invite them to connect. Look for ways to be helpful, opportunities for shared interests, and people you already have in common by scanning for data related to their lives outside of work. Find out where they went to college. Look online and try to figure out where they volunteer. Explore LinkedIn to discover any real-life friends you have in common.

Set up a Google alert at https://www.google.com /alerts and spy on your company, your boss, your CEO, and even the HR leader or recruiter who hired you. Keep an eye out for opportunities to talk with your new team about hot-button issues, challenges, and industry stories.

Every new job becomes an old job at some point. Relationships don't just make work easier; they make work bearable during the tough times. So cement relationships as soon as you can, and be welcomed by encouraging faces on the first day of work, even if you have to find them on your own.

THE FUTURE OF HR IS
ACTUALLY INTERESTING

I've shown you how HR sucks (though you probably already knew it—or you wouldn't have picked up this book), but now I'm here to tell you that HR is changing like every other industry. As work changes—with automation creeping into the workforce, cost-cutting measures in place, and fewer and fewer people working as full-time employees—the duties and responsibilities of the people who remain in human resources will look different. What's the future of HR, and does it matter to you? I think it does.

First, the future of HR is automated and digitized. Technology will disrupt the department, and then hopefully improve it. There aren't robots coming for those jobs. But there are chatbots, algorithms, and outsourced service providers. The experience will be less human, requiring you to work harder when said technology fails. And the remaining HR professionals will probably fall into two camps: boots-on-the-ground project managers who do a bit of everything, from employee relations to troubleshooting with tech, and coaches who focus solely on organizational health and psychology.

The first role is entirely tactical. When your paycheck is wrong, or your benefits need to be adjusted, the future HR professional will be your level-2 support once you've tried and failed to solve your own problems via the Internet. And they'll be available to chat on video or maybe in real life if you are fighting with your boss.

The second role is strategic. Companies will hire psychologists and data scientists to optimize everything from worker training to employee health. We already live in an era of surveillance. Companies use programs to read your email, watch your Internet usage, and even monitor your personal phone if you're plugged into corporate Wi-Fi. So don't be surprised when your employers use the data you give them to work you to the brink of death in the name of productivity.

How then do you fix work and be your own HR in an era of such rapid change? Well, whether you're a full-time employee or on a limited contract with a company, run your life like the leader you're meant to be. Ask yourself what traditional HR used to ask: What are your goals from work? Why are you here? How do the activities at work fit into your life story?

If you don't have good answers, future HR teams and their corporate overlords will eat you alive.

In many ways, it's best to operate as if the future is now. Guard against intrusions into your personal time and prioritize well-being to make yourself a better and more productive worker. Invest in your education to earn more opportunities. Fix your money to be less stressed and desperate when accepting a job. If you get your life together, you will force companies to offer you better opportunities—and benefits—if they want to attract and keep you as a worker.

Finally, it doesn't matter what the current or future state of HR looks like unless you understand *why* you work. Once you know your purpose, it's easier to say no to emotionally volatile cultures and instead say yes to opportunities where you can learn and grow. Being your own HR leader is the best and most essential way to fix work because it takes power away from a bureaucratic department with no consistent job duties and puts the responsibility of having a good day at work—or getting over a bad week at work—squarely in your own hands.

No one can make you work at a lousy job without your consent, not even HR. Stop wondering what the hell is wrong with HR—like my seatmate in 3B—and work on claiming your employee experience as your own, as if HR doesn't matter. Because, frankly, it doesn't.

7

Job Search 101

HOW TO BE A SECRET
JOB SEARCH SPY

I have a theory that the truth is never told
during the nine-to-five hours.

—HUNTER S. THOMPSON

Think back on what prompted you to look for your
last job. You might have been angry. Maybe you were
poached by a competitor. Perhaps it was time to leave.

A friend of mine named Jake wasn't looking for work
until his company took his office away and made him sit
in a cubicle. The HR department and local facilities team
made a "strategic decision" to reduce expenses by creating
an open floor plan. They traded privacy and sunshine for
circular bullpens, benches, and enhanced cubicle farms
without divided walls for privacy. They should know better.
They *do* know better.

The verdict is in: open-office environments are noisy and disruptive. Workers are often distracted all day long—and you are likely one of them. You might wear noise-canceling headphones to drown out the sound of your coworkers. And when it's all too much, maybe you retreat to a conference room, lobby, stairwells, or even the germy bathroom to have an uninterrupted moment of focus.

Jake saw the writing on the wall and asked for my help.

"How do I search for work without being overheard? I don't want to get caught looking because of the open office."

Good question. Open offices may make it particularly challenging, but in general, people want to know how to find a new job while they still have one. It's a valid question. It's not easy to conduct a confidential job search and maintain your anonymity until the last moment. And everybody wants to know how long it will take. What if you find nothing better?

If you are looking for work but can't risk your current job, take heart. So is everybody else. It takes a hell of a lot of courage to look for a job. In the perfect world, employees should have the strength to express any concerns or misgivings to management, and management would respond in turn to make things better. They would work with their supervisor or the HR department to overcome obstacles and find solutions that benefit everyone. And they would be the change they wish to see—fixing work by sticking around and seeing things through. But that's a lot to ask of people who are overworked, underpaid, and enrolled in shoddy health care.

In the real world, workers quit long before they give their two-week notice. They quit on a Tuesday night when the CEO gets a bonus but everybody else earns a 3.2 percent merit increase as a thank-you for working nights and weekends. They quit on a Monday morning when the weekend wasn't long enough and the week ahead feels bleak. And they quit in the community kitchen when people don't clean up after themselves or do the dishes.

Whatever the reason, it's important to remember that no job is forever. Whether you work as an executive or a busboy, everybody quits. Turnover happens. And very few can openly search for a new role while still maintaining a positive and professional relationship to their employer. It doesn't matter where you work. Many companies will fire you on the spot—or at least make your life much more difficult—if you are honest about looking for a new job.

The hospitality sector is especially ruthless. I have a family member who worked as a bartender at a fast-casual chain of restaurants. Every single job search was done with a mix of paranoia and fear. She told me that if her supervisor found out, he'd take away her hours—like he did to the other servers who dared to look for better-paying and more flexible jobs.

Unless you were born rich or have unlimited resources (which makes it possible to withstand prolonged unemployment), you must be cautious when applying to jobs while still employed. But it *is* possible to conduct a job search with integrity so you don't shortchange your company—or yourself. You can explore the job market, find something different, and accept a new role without all that drama. Here's how.

YOUR JOB SEARCH IS NOBODY'S BUSINESS BUT YOURS

Never assume that your job search is confidential. You can trust doctors, lawyers, and clergy. Mostly. But everybody else is suspect. The moment you open your mouth (or open up a browser on your phone), you have relinquished the right to privacy. And if you want to keep your search confidential, tell as few people as possible, which includes your best friend at the office.

You might think I am paranoid and say, "My colleagues are supportive. We're like a family around here. They've got my back." Sure. But if you're so close to these people, why are you leaving? Also, your work BFF does *not* have your back. Amanda in accounting might pinky swear that she will never tell a soul about your upcoming interviews.

The truth is, Amanda is a stone-cold liar, and there is nothing she loves more than to stroll over to the HR department and stir up trouble.

And it's important to watch yourself online because Mark Zuckerberg most definitely does *not* have your back. They are tracking you—tech companies, advertising agencies, and publishers of all ilk. Even organizations that guarantee anonymity and confidentiality today can update their terms of service tomorrow.

So, you might be wondering, if you can't trust anyone, not even Siri, how does one look for a job discreetly? The answer is to go through someone at your desired company rather than apply for positions posted online. That's right. Go analog in a digital world.

First, get a pen and jot down a list of dream companies like you are a boy-crazy middle schooler. Start dreaming in a safe and private place (e.g., not at work) about the companies where you'd like to be. These are your corporate crushes—the businesses you think about when you close your eyes at night. Maybe it's Apple or a local start-up. Perhaps you dream about working for a nonprofit. Whatever it is, stalk them like they're a boy named Corey Zywicki in your eighth-grade science class.

Then do your due diligence and read reviews about the company on Yelp, Google Reviews, Trustpilot, and Angie's List. Use LinkedIn's search bar to find mentions of the company in posts and groups. Don't just look for clues on the CEO or basic financial information that allows you to skate through an interview. Go to Instagram and read comments from haters. Get a complete picture of the news, gossip, and stories about crappy leaders on ex-employee blogs.

But before you do this, please make sure you are off the clock and not using your company's Wi-Fi! If you don't have access to technology at home, go to the public library. (And while you're there, spend some time browsing around the stacks of books and getting to know the joint. Librarians have missed you.)

Once you have stalked your dream companies, it's time to dance. For many of us, it never feels right to ask someone for help. But now is not the time to be shy. If you know *anybody* who works at one of your preferred companies, connect with them via phone or personal email. You don't have to know them well. Maybe you met them through church, at school, or because their kid plays with yours on a traveling soccer league. It doesn't matter. Call them up, send them an email, or pull them aside at one of those horrible all-day tournaments. Just try to connect on a human level.

Here's the secret about forming a connection: it only takes four minutes of chitchat (or one round of email) to know whether someone will be helpful. Did I make up that four-minute fact? I sure did. But does it feel right? You know it does. That's because helpful people use positive body language and have warmer tones in their voice. They ask open-ended questions, even in email. Almost immediately, there's an implied invitation to keep the conversation going.

"In person," says Nick Morgan, author of *Can You Hear Me?: How to Connect with People in a Virtual World*, "we make up our minds unconsciously in less than thirty seconds whether someone we meet is friend or foe, helpful or not. Online, the process takes a little longer. If you want some help, offer to do something for them; the principle of reciprocity is very powerful online."

If you get the green light, ask for advice on how to apply and interview for a job at the organization with discretion. That last part is the key. Try saying, "I'm not really in the market for a new position, but I am interested in your organization's culture and would love to learn more. Is there someone I can talk to confidentially?" We know nothing is confidential, but using the word *confidential* is the perfect verbal reminder that the stakes are high. If you can't get a name, ask for an introduction to the HR or recruiting team.

If you don't know anybody at your dream company (or nobody wants to help you), you're stuck like the rest of us. You must play the game of applying for jobs online, which exposes you to a little risk.

And about 35 percent of people find work through job sites and online portals. But once you become part of a formal hiring process, all bets are off when it comes to confidentiality and discretion.

Some recruiters and HR professionals are sloppy. They

"ghost" candidates—interviewing them one day, ignoring them the next. Or they have big mouths, make mistakes, and blurt out private information at the wrong time that winds up in the ears of your boss. I can't tell you how many times I've been at events where recruiters reveal individual secrets gleaned from interviews. Forget sophisticated European data protection laws—we need protection from Christina, a local talent acquisition specialist who vents about her job at networking events and accidentally tips off your current employer that you're looking around. This is why you must stay vigilant and proactively remind everybody involved—from the recruiter to the hiring professional—that you respect and admire your current employer, so your job search is confidential. Say that. Short and sweet.

Finally, if you do get an offer, don't let your confidentiality guard down. A lot can go wrong between the time you sign an offer letter and the day you walk in the building and shake hands with your new boss. Employers still check references. Some do it before the offer, but most do it post-offer. Never lie, and don't omit information about your history that can be found in a courthouse. When asked for references, only share the names of individuals who would give you a kidney—or at least will stay quiet and support you. And make sure you give them a heads-up that you've listed them as a reference. If you don't have those people in your life, start making some friends before you embark on a confidential job search.

And, if worse comes to worst, and your boss finds out that you were applying to other jobs, you can say, "I am sorry you found out, but I am curious about the market and wanted to explore. I tried to work with the interviewing team to keep the process confidential out of respect for you and this company. I am still committed to this job." It's okay to put yourself first. And if your company is angry that you took control of your career and conducted a confidential, thoughtful, and considered job search, it doesn't deserve you in the first place.

HOW EFFING LONG WILL THIS TAKE?

How long will it take to find a job? Who knows? But if you don't fix yourself and figure out the source of your unhappiness, it *will* take forever. No company or boss can ever make you happy. You will be a depressed adult who guzzles antidepressants and wonders why you are tired, pessimistic, unable to run through the airport without stopping a dozen times to catch your breath. (Okay, that was me.)

So how long will it take *you* to find a job? The honest answer is that it takes as long as it takes. A quick and dirty job search gets you a quick and dirty job—just like the one you have, with the same problems but a different group of colleagues. A more fulfilling life, with a balanced approach to work, comes from first changing your mindset and your habits.

My business coach, Jesse Itzler, is the author of *Living with a SEAL: 31 Days Training with the Toughest Man on the Planet*. He taught me that successful executives are scheduled and organized. For people like that, there are no "zero" days where you waste time and miss opportunities to get one step closer to your goals. When you wake up, your time should be accounted for on a calendar. Every moment matters, from the minute you wake until the second you go to bed. You don't have to schedule every bathroom break, but your days should be planned and intentional.

Jesse encouraged me to put down my phone and get serious about time management. He recommended a big desk calendar to plan out themes for the year with a particular emphasis on the weeks and months when it's easy to waste a lot of time. Then he taught me how to visualize and plan each day through specific daily and evening rituals. I paid good money for his coaching, but thankfully I did because it changed my life. And here's a lesson I learned that applies to you: scheduling your day is the key to a shorter, faster, confidential job search.

Instead of falling down rabbit holes and doing dodgy "research" on the Internet, get systematic and intentional. Plan out your days. Start by scheduling buckets of time for the big stuff like networking with integrity, talking to people you trust about how to apply for jobs, mentoring younger workers, and volunteering within your industry.

Then block out specific time to complete applications, read industry news on the Internet, and track your progress on a spreadsheet where you list each company you've applied to and what you've heard back. Make the time you spend on the Internet matter. And then, when you're done, get off the Internet. You've completed that task. Don't look back.

Need more ideas on how to schedule your time and shorten your job search?

Leaders are voracious readers, and they hire people just like them. That's called the halo effect. Make time in your week to read something that isn't on the Internet—either fiction or nonfiction. You pick; there are no bad choices. Even comic books will give you a competitive edge in the interview process by making you a more appealing human being with a different perspective on life. When I interviewed for my ill-fated job at Pfizer, one of the panelists talked to me about modern art. I'm a dilettante and can talk about just anything, but it was a stroke of luck that I spent lots of time in and around art museums. Reading books and listening to docents talk about the works of Jeff Koons and Chuck Close gave me a competitive edge with that interviewer.

Also, this may sound counterintuitive, but you'll shorten your job search if you help someone else find a job. Most people think they're HR experts because they can format and edit a résumé. Don't be basic and suggest the same old help that anybody can offer. Open up your LinkedIn profile, connect other job seekers to recruiters and leaders who have been helpful to you, or simply listen to someone else's depressing stories. Connecting with other unemployed people can seem like a time suck, but it's another aspect of doing the premortem. If you can figure out what other people are doing wrong, you can avoid mistakes before you make them.

And lastly, you can't be a legitimate contender for a job unless your mind-set is calm and deliberate. When I was a hiring manager, I could always tell the serious candidates from the desperate individuals who sat in their basement all day long on a computer. Serious applicants are intentional about where they send their résumés. They don't apply for multiple jobs on a website hoping for a hit. And they always include a personalized cover letter, even if they don't think I'll read it. When they show up to the interview, they are in control. They don't babble or get lost in thoughts. They are practiced, measured, and know what's happening within themselves. Desperate candidates think the world is against them, worry about being judged, and feel like victims of circumstances. They've given up on themselves. Instead of having a strategy, they wing it. And your job search will take forever if you wing it.

I recognize that looking for work sucks. It's a time-consuming process involving lots of risks. But unless you win the lottery, you've got to play the game. You can complain about it—and goodness knows I love to complain—but you should also manage your expectations and work hard to make it easy for someone to hire you.

INTERVIEW LIKE A CHAMP

Let's talk a little more about that much-dreaded interview. There's no point in looking for work if you aren't prepared to stick every interview like an Olympic gold gymnast. Unfortunately, people fail for stupid reasons.

I'm just going to say it: people blow it because they are intellectually and emotionally sloppy. They're scared of the process and haven't learned how to control their emotions. They can't make eye contact when someone talks to them, or their minds are somewhere else—thinking about bills, children, even grocery lists.

Don't be like those people. When you fail to show up mentally, it presents a challenge to the hiring team. Your résumé might be memorable, and your work experience could be exactly what the company needs, but nobody is saying hell yes to your candidacy. They'll keep looking, and prolong the hiring process, until they find someone they love.

Once, I interviewed a young man who showed up for his nine o'clock interview and asked how long this would take because he had to leave at nine thirty for work. I was like, *Don't let me get in your way, buddy.*

Then there's the woman who came in for an early morning interview after accidentally filling in her eyebrows with a purple eyeliner pencil instead of brown. That's an honest mistake, but it's a costly one when you're applying for a job where "attention to detail" matters.

Or my favorite: the woman who Skyped in for an interview from a tiny office at work and was always looking up to see if her colleagues were watching. *Yes, dammit, they're watching you. I'm watching you watch them.* It was all very meta.

To nail an interview and speed up the timeline, be an active player in the process. If a recruiter asks you to interview at a time that doesn't work for you—early morning, late at night, during your weekly staff meeting—put yourself first and say no. You have agency. Suggest alternative times. Otherwise, you're coming at this in a half-assed way, and it's over before it's begun.

Next, look fresh. I'm not asking you to get a makeover, but I am asking you to respect the process enough to impress the hiring team. Yes, there is a beauty bias in our culture. Yes, our interview processes are flawed and based on random first impressions that don't correlate to success. But you can nail the interview by wearing what you'd wear to have lunch with Oprah. Would you throw on old clothes to meet the richest woman in America? Flip-flops? Leggings that are worn out and show your underwear? I don't think so.

One middle-aged dude interviewed for a customer service manager job in the nicest version of Harley gear that I've ever seen. We offered him the role because he'd probably wear that to have a burger with Oprah and her best friend Gayle. And sure, I've hired plenty of people in golf shirts and khakis—which is the standard dressy-business-casual attire for white men everywhere—but I've also selected individuals with tattoos and piercings who look phenomenal and would kill it at tea with Oprah any day of the week.

If you ever wonder what to wear for an interview, it's simple. Be *you* on your terms. Just freshen it up and try to impress the most successful woman on the planet. Don't bankrupt yourself by buying expensive accessories or pretend to be someone else in luxury labels you can't afford. Oprah respects a deal at TJ Maxx.

Once you have your look down it's time to get focused. Turn off your phone, don't wear a watch that beeps and buzzes, and leave your work at work. I've had candidates read text messages on their watches, ask me to stop talking so they can take a call because it's their boss, or call me the wrong name because they're thinking about the last email message they've received. Are they nervous? Sure. But could they prepare themselves more effectively? Absolutely. Put your body and mind where your heart already is—your future with a new job.

Finally, seal the deal by asking for feedback before you walk out the door. My favorite questions to ask: "Do you have any feedback for me on this interview? Are there any other questions you'd like to ask before I leave? Anything that causes concerns?" Put it out there. Be brave. And then shut up. Let them tell you they don't like the gap on your résumé, your job history, or your lack of an MBA. If you've done a premortem on your life at any point, you'll already know the deficiency, and you'll be prepared to address it.

And please, I cannot stress this enough, don't ask when you'll hear from them. That puts you in a position of weakness. Instead, nail the interview by asking *how* and *when* <u>you</u> can follow up. Get specific. Listen hard to the answer. If there's no timeline, gently push and let them know you will call or email within a week. If there is a timeline, that's fantastic. Repeat it. Acknowledge it. Shake on it. Look them in the eye so they honor it. Follow up the same day with a thank-you note.

If the recruiting team or hiring manager doesn't meet their commitment to you, follow up three times, with each interaction six days apart. If you still don't hear, let it go. Why six days? It's less than a week, allows for weekends, and gives you a mental road map of the next few weeks. More important, it also permits you to let things go.

The goal of an interview is to make it easy to hire you. Show up emotionally and physically. Wear your best Oprah outfit. Bring your whole self to the conversation. Ask for feedback. *That's* how you nail this process and emerge with a job offer. Everything else is just a waste of time.

THE WAITING IS THE HARDEST PART

I believe there are two types of job seekers: smart and squishy. *Smart* job seekers understand that the world is a mix of good and evil, harmony and chaos, right and wrong. They know that life throws curveballs, so they don't stand in the middle of the plate and make themselves a target. Instead, they learn the game and try to play.

Squishy job seekers believe the world is a mix of good and bad—not because of physics or evolutionary psychology but because of something they did or didn't do in their lifetimes. The world is either delightful or horrible. When life throws them curveballs, they don't learn to catch or step out of the way. They will take a pitch to the face and walk away with two black eyes, all while telling you about their fractured childhood.

If you are like me, you've been both *smart* and *squishy* at different stages of your life. You were squishy with your in-laws but grew smart when you realized there was no appeasing people who will never like you. You were squishy with a pushy friend who didn't understand boundaries but smart with the next person who tested your patience.

The time for being squishy is over, especially while looking for work and waiting to hear back about the results of an interview. When it feels like you don't have many opportunities and life has let you down, you only have one option: move forward.

Maybe you keep interviewing for jobs and never hear back. Perhaps you wore your best Oprah outfit and impressed the hell out of a team that has since ghosted you. Maybe you started freelancing in the gig economy, but nobody is responding to your proposals. You can be *squishy* and wonder why this keeps happening to you, or you can be *smart* and watch for what's next.

Being smart means admitting you lack control over external situations—interviews, discussions, negotiations—but still retain control over your attitudes, feelings, beliefs, and spending. It also means keeping current events in perspective and not diving into the past or flashing forward to the future to derive meaning from things happening today.

Being smart requires being brave and creative, like my friend Damian, who was so nervous about his professional job search that he purposely pursued a job *he was guaranteed to get* but *would never accept* just to practice what it's like to interview, make mistakes, and succeed.

Read that again. Damian looked for a job he would be offered but would never accept so he could practice interviewing. You can do that, too. Head down to a local retailer or restaurant chain, apply for a job that you wouldn't take in a million years, and then practice interviewing. Heck, go apply at a big corporation. When you get the offer, celebrate but turn it down.

Squishy job seekers stay with their pain and self-doubt because it's easier than confronting their fears and making a plan. My buddy Arjun called me after a series of interviews and told me that he felt *unemployable*. He wanted to know if it was something about him that made him a loser. Was it in his DNA to suck? Could other people sense his impostor syndrome?

These are questions to explore with a therapist, not a career coach, but I will say that nobody should feel that way about themselves. The squishy feelings of desperation and depression have a way of becoming a new normal if you don't tackle them head-on with the proper tools and resources. Research therapy and counseling. They can help.

Squishy job seekers are also masters of self-sabotage. My friend Marie tried to talk herself into sticking with a job she hated because nobody called her back after a dozen interviews. I don't have a PhD in psychology, so I'm not sure why she put herself through that torture and then gave up. But I'm glad she finally called me for help.

Marie and I reverse-engineered her job search, and it turns out that she assumed most jobs were terrible and would discriminate against her. Interviewers can tell when you're squishy, assume bad intent, and lack enthusiasm about the job.

Smart or squishy, waiting during a job search is the hardest part for everyone. Lots of ruminating thoughts happen while you're sitting around, caught up in a negative feedback loop, and making up stories about why you suck. The likelihood that you'll be rejected is high, and, yet, you're like everybody else looking for work and holding out hope. You might ask yourself, Is it worse to be rejected for a job straightaway or hear nothing at all?

I think rejection is rejection—whether you get it in the form of email, a letter, or silence. But you are doing yourself a disservice by sitting around at your current job hitting refresh on your in-box. If they offer you a job, you'll know about it. Your future employer won't just email.

They'll call, send a text, and probably shower you with a bunch of company swag. If they can't find you, they'll shoot up some flares and send out a search party.

Smart people know this.

They go on interviews, give it their best effort, and keep things in perspective. They fix work by fixing themselves. The hard part is over. They took a risk and placed a bet. Smart people aren't desperate for a job because they've already fixed their finances, acted as their own talent agent, and prepared themselves for rejection. Smart people do the work of being emotionally regulated adults who have lives outside of work, continuing to learn, explore new ideas outside their careers, and remain cautious about getting too excited over things they cannot control. Smart people are squishy and vulnerable like the rest of us, but they bounce back faster because they have perspective and live in the present—with friends, family, colleagues, neighbors, and even animals who depend on them to be focused and emotionally grounded.

Squishy people can get smart by adopting the tools and advice peppered throughout this book. Learn from past mistakes using a premortem, create a budget so you're never desperate for income, and analyze rejection for what it is—a bet that didn't pay off—and what it isn't—a sweeping indictment of you as a human being.

We live in a work-obsessed culture where it's easy to confuse your worth as a human being with your work. I'm here to tell you that your value as a citizen of this planet has nothing to do with your career. You matter so long as you are kind, helpful, and empathetic. You make a difference because you care for your neighbors and friends. And there is nothing to be gained from beating up on yourself because you didn't get a job. It's just a job. It matters, but it doesn't. Move forward. Do the next thing.

Waiting sucks. Rejection also sucks. It will always be that way. But don't make it worse by being unkind to yourself over a situation you can't control. You're so much smarter than that.

A JOB OFFER: THE FINAL FRONTIER

If you're one of the lucky people who successfully conducts a confidential job search while working a full-time job elsewhere and gets an offer, congratulations! You've navigated a complex maze of drama and emotions. You deserve more than a new job. You deserve a PhD in industrial psychology. And now that you have an offer in hand, you have three options: accept it without negotiating, negotiate the heck out of it, or reject it.

Let's start at the beginning. Why would you accept the offer without negotiating? Well, because it's good. You trust the company and it gave you everything you asked for. You are happy. That's it. End of story. Good luck with your new role.

Why negotiate? Listen, there are people out there who tell you to negotiate everything. You should never leave money on the table, and always negotiate for one more thing—even if it's just one extra day of PTO.

I once spoke on a panel with an executive coach named Ching Valdezco. She is an executive who helps professionals communicate, speak, and influence more effectively. Ching was apoplectic over the amount of money that women and POC leave on the table during salary negotiations, and she pushed attendees to overcome the fear of asking by adopting a feeling of professional entitlement.

Her perspective was right out of a New York City or Silicon Valley boardroom: You work hard. You are a leader, a fighter, and a champion. Run your life like a business. Fight for what's yours.

After listening to Ching, I was inspired to ask for more. (Too bad I'm my own boss.)

Negotiating a job offer is one of the scariest things you can do, but it's also one of the most rewarding things when it comes to personal development. The fear of asking for more is that someone might say no, but, if you don't ask, nobody can say yes.

There are scenarios in which you're not going to get a dime more than what's offered on paper. Some companies will give you an offer letter and say this is their *first*, *best*, and *final* offer. That's because organizations are trying to eliminate racial and gender inequality. A job pays what it pays because it's been researched and integrated into a company-wide compensation philosophy. If they negotiate, it might set their whole system backward and reintroduce pay inequality.

Many executive coaches will tell you that a first, best, and final offer is a lie. They will encourage you to ask for more. But I think it's worth investigating your potential employer on Glassdoor, Kununu, Reddit, or even Fairygodboss. Poke around and ask questions about process, intent, and even the company's compensation philosophy. Get the inside scoop before trying to negotiate your base compensation or bonus.

Finally, why would you flat-out reject an offer? Well, just because you interviewed for a job doesn't mean you have to accept it. Maybe you were using it to gain leverage with your current employer, or maybe you learned something about the company during the hiring process that gave you pause. You might have even discovered something about yourself during the process and changed course.

You should never take a job if you know the atmosphere is toxic. You'll never earn enough to compensate for the emotional toll on your head and in your heart. Similarly, never accept an offer from an organization that doesn't align with your values. It's easy to rationalize and pretend values don't matter, but they do. They might ask you to produce work in the name of a person or a cause that doesn't align with your beliefs. And you should not take a job that makes you feel demeaned, degraded, or nickel-and-dimed. Your humanity is at the core of everything you do. If a company doesn't see your intrinsic worth now, it won't see it. Ever.

But the good news is that job offers are almost always positive.

Remember my friend Jake from earlier in the chapter? The one who looked for new work when they took his office away? He interviewed at half a dozen companies and walked out of three interviews when he saw people working in cubicles. When he finally got an offer, it was for a similar job and title and no raise. But he got an office. And want to know what's even better? He negotiated a commitment to keep his office for at least two years. If the building underwent renovations and converted to an open-office floor plan, they'd find him another place to sit with four walls and a door. If Jake can get a new job with a twenty-four-month guarantee of being in an office, what can you get?

WHEN DOES THIS JOB SEARCH TORTURE END?

There are career experts out there who will tell you to "always be looking" for work. I think that's exhausting, boring advice. Ignore it.

My honest take is to "always be living." Go out on a limb, try to learn (at least a little) each day, and always grow from your mistakes. Manage your money, be an advocate for yourself, and master the ins and outs of being rejected.

Living life well is the *best* way to get a job. Be open to opportunities, available to talk if it feels right, and helpful when someone else needs a job. Don't be the person on a perpetual job search. You'll burn out and become squishy. Instead, make real connections. Be someone who cares for others and is worth caring about. It's really the only way to make it through this lifetime with any hope of happiness.

8

Quittin' Time

LEAVE WITH DIGNITY
AND MONEY IN YOUR POCKET

I'm not running away, I'm moving on.

—IRVINE WELSH

My baby boomer parents drilled it into me at a young age that you don't quit your job unless you have another one lined up. This was a rule without exceptions. Is your workplace culture toxic? Has your boss shit on your dreams? Even if it's the worst job on the planet, you do not quit. My dad believed work doesn't exist to make you happy—it exists to put food on the table and pay your bills. My mom said they don't call it work because it's fun, they call it work because it's hard.

All these years later, I still carry their advice in my bones.

Just recently, I worked with a client in Silicon Valley

who asked me to spend time with the HR team and assist an important transformation project. The corporate headquarters was an open-office concept with workbenches that felt like an airplane hangar. Many of the employees ducked out and had meetings at coffeehouses and restaurants in order to actually get things done.

My seat was across from the VP of communications, who clearly displayed signs of being emotionally disengaged from her job. Nobody worked as hard as she did, but it was also clear that nothing made her happy. There were always obstacles, never opportunities. And she was a hoarder and kept twelve pairs of shoes under her desk. Clogs. Boots. Flats. Sneakers. Strappy heels. Pumps. Wedges. Peep-toes. Rain boots. Espadrilles. Flip-flops. Ankle booties. There was barely any room under her workstation for her feet. Whenever I got up from my desk to get a cup of coffee, she'd take my absence as an opportunity to push her shoes into my workspace. I'd come back from the kitchen and have to push her shoes back under the partition. We played this game for weeks.

And while she had every single pair of shoes from Zappos under her desk, this VP always seemed to leave her laptop power cord at home. When I would leave for lunch, she'd grab my charger and plug it into her computer. Once, on a Friday, she left work and took that power cord home. As the weeks progressed, the shoe lady grew more and more agitated. Sometimes, when nobody except the two of us were around, she'd sing musical theater songs while reading email. At other times, she would interrupt me while I was on the phone during conference calls to ask questions that were totally unimportant.

I tried to call a truce by presenting her with a gift. I bought her a book, wrapped it in a charming gift bag, and gave it to her on a Friday before a long weekend. She unwrapped the book and said, "Wow. Another business book to sit on a pile of unread business books that I'll never read." The truce was over before it started.

I was so taken aback that I almost quit that client on the spot. I didn't fly to Tijuana and leave my corporate HR job at Pfizer just to work with another uptight woman. But there was another voice in my head—the voice of my parents—who told me that I couldn't quit this consulting gig until I had another one lined up.

Instead of walking out, I just shook my head and wished her well in my heart. We shoved shoes for a few more weeks until my consulting engagement was over. Then I cashed my final check and went on my merry way.

Were my parents right about not quitting a job before you have a job? It depends. Overall, they meant well, just like so many parents before them. My dad's career at the phone company was never fulfilling, so his advice came from a place of pain. And my mom had only a GED. On a whim, she took the Chicago Police Officer Exam. When she was admitted to the academy, we couldn't believe it. Nobody thought she could do it—except *her*. My mom studied hard, learned the ins and outs of police work, and pushed herself to meet the physical requirements of the job. She worked the overnight shift as a beat cop for a decade but left that job and never worked again.

Now, hating your job isn't the same as lacking a work ethic. My parents worked their butts off. My dad had child support payments to make and walked miles to the train station so he could commute into the city of Chicago—to a job he seemed to hate—and provide for our family. My mom worked the midnight shift while raising children and managing the politics of being a police officer.

But work burned them out, and I think they never found their groove as adults. I wonder—why the heck did it have to be this way? Why didn't they quit and follow their dreams? Why don't *you* quit?

Listen, I know why you don't leave. I've heard it all before. You can't afford it. You are afraid of change. You suffer from impostor syndrome. You feel guilty for leaving your colleagues behind.

All of that can be true, and you can still quit your job. Maybe not today. But someday. And you can start planning for someday right now.

QUIT YER COMPLAINING

Nothing is more satisfying than quitting a bad job. I won't lie—it feels great to turn in a letter of resignation and count down the days on your phone's calendar app.

But if you can't quit your job this instant, you can quit *other* things that led you to the crummy job in the first place.

Early in my coaching career, a woman named Helen contacted me. She hated everything about her job but couldn't afford to quit without another opportunity lined up. It's a common dilemma. Many people have financial challenges and the new job must pay precisely the same amount of money or more. Not a dime less. Helen couldn't pay for my career coaching, but she wanted free advice on how to find another job—fast.

I told her, "The job market always favors candidates who are serious and specific about their career interests. If you want a job that pays well, you'll need to work with someone to explore how you got into your bad job in the first place."

"You don't seem to be very good at career coaching," Helen replied.

I tried to end the conversation by telling Helen that going to therapy and learning problem-solving strategies were probably the best ways to fix work problems, but she cut me off. "I'm stressed and tired. Nobody will listen to me. Nobody will help me. I just want to quit my job and take a break."

Unfortunately for Helen, there was no cavalry coming, nor an easy answer to appease her concerns. The only person who could give Helen permission to slow down, sit with her discomfort at work, and figure out exactly what's wrong with the current job before she rolls into the next was Helen. And she wasn't patient enough to do it.

Helen's LinkedIn profile hasn't been updated in a few years. Her work history ends with that bad job. Honestly, I'm not surprised. She thought "putting yourself first" meant quitting, but that's wrong. Putting yourself first means knowing why things are going wrong and crafting a strategy to turn it around—professionally, personally, financially, and emotionally.

Walking out of a bad job without a plan rarely solves anything. You get a black stain on your record from your previous company. Employers want to know why you left your last job. And you can't ask your former colleagues to be dishonest. Besides, people don't lie very well. That's why I never tell someone it's okay to quit a job without another one lined up. It's simply not in my DNA. Instead, keep working while you conduct a speedy job search (as outlined in chapter 7) and explore your culpability in having a bad job in the first place.

If you're feeling stressed, work fewer hours. Be a slacker. Nobody will notice. It's counterintuitive, but the more time you spend at your desk or in meetings, the less likely you are to be productive. Nobody ever felt better by reading one more email or answering one more question on a group conference call. Learn to say no, set boundaries, and schedule time for administrative work, creative work, project work, and downtime to rest your brain. Get up and go outside for lunch. There's no reason why you need to eat that turkey sandwich and side salad at your desk.

If you're feeling confrontational and aggressive, leave work early and go work out. Don't beat up on yourself or a coworker. Beat a punching bag. Let off some steam and take a break from whatever is bothering you. If you're worried about working less and getting in trouble, quit those long hours and dare them to fire you in a gracious way. Pivot away from work and embrace your emotional health. Nobody gets fired for getting more sleep and being happier; people are fired for being jerks.

As we've been practicing, you must fix what's broken about life before you try to fix work by quitting.

Even if you have cash set aside to cover a prolonged period of unemployment, hang on to your job until you find a new one. Many jobs are being automated and digitized. The job you quit today may not exist in another two years. Your skills might become obsolete during your job search, and potential employers can't trust that you are staying current and learning new things like you would if you were employed and immersed in training programs or management platforms.

Many people quit work and find themselves lost in the gig economy, taking on freelance jobs or accepting contract assignments in hopes that they will go temp-to-perm. Whatever the case, most individuals don't have a business plan for their lives. They leave a job for all the right reasons, and with the best of intentions, but continue to feel just as lost and helpless as the day they quit. This is why it's so important to have the next thing lined up before you quit.

If you don't yet, here are a few other things I suggest quitting instead of your job.

Quit winging your finances. You can't tell your boss to take this job and shove it if you are broke. Build wealth so you can be choosier about your next job.

Quit doing a half-assed job search. Throw your whole ass into that search, baby. Then leave when you land a job with your dream company.

Quit feeling attached to an organization and a group of people who aren't your family and will never love you back. We spend so much of our life at work, which is problematic enough, so set up limits on your attention. Instead of obsessing about workplace gossip, obsess about yourself and your individual needs. If that sounds too touchy-feely, obsess about the people at home who miss you when you're gone.

Quit giving in to the emotional turmoil in your head and heart. You're not a prisoner, you are an employee. Use the tools I've given you to anticipate what might happen if you quit your job without another one lined up. Call your employee assistance program, talk to someone you trust, or go to therapy. Fix yourself.

Quit making excuses that keep you stuck in a job that eats your soul alive. The circumstances of life can be cruel, but you don't have to be an accomplice to brutality.

Understand why you keep making the same mistakes in your career, and resolve them.

Finally, quit complaining.

○ ○ ○

Do I think you should quit your stressful, unfulfilling, or miserable job? Of course. Eventually. But stick it out until you have another job, and work on yourself in the meanwhile. All jobs are toxic jobs if you quit without addressing what's broken in the first place.

BE A BADASS AND
ASK FOR SEVERANCE PAY

Here's an HR secret most of us would never admit out loud: we will pay almost anybody to leave the company as long as they sign a release and waiver declaring they won't sue. That's right—we will give you extra money when you quit if you ask for it and promise not to get a lawyer involved down the road.

Now, this isn't to be confused with tech companies and prominent retailers who offer an "exit bonus," which pays workers to leave after the first thirty days if it doesn't work out. For example, the US-based retailer Zappos writes workers a check if they willingly raise their hand and say, "Nah, brah, this isn't for me."

I love exit bonuses. I think it's a good idea to pay someone to leave whether they go after three weeks, three months, or three years. Turnover is healthy and creates opportunities for an organization to grow by gaining new people, fresh ideas, and positive energy. Exit bonuses drive growth by encouraging employees to leave when they no longer feel they're contributing. They're great. But that's not what I'm really talking about.

What I'm discussing is severance pay: money paid to an employee when she's laid off. But severance pay isn't just for people who are made redundant in a corporate restructuring. Depending on your company's policies, you might qualify for a payout if you leave the organization of your own accord. You just have to ask.

Have you ever wondered why your underperforming VP of marketing sticks around when the numbers are bad? It's because she's waiting to be fired. Even if she's miserable and can barely get out of bed in the morning, she's not going anywhere. She will drive her company car to the office, sulk in her Herman Miller chair, and wait for somebody above her to make a strategic decision about her future because that's how it's written into her contract. She negotiated a year's worth of her salary upon exit and is waiting for the CEO to approach her and say, "It's over." They'll pay her to go.

That will never happen to you. But there is another option: **ask for a severance payment before you resign.** If you've been conducting a confidential job search, as I outlined in the previous chapter, nobody knows that you've been looking for work and have a new role lined up. Use that discretion to your advantage like my client Tamara, who found a phenomenal job that paid 20 percent more than her current salary.

She didn't write a letter of resignation straightaway. She knew that her VP of sales had recently been replaced and the company had restructured the entire sales and marketing department. So she pulled out the company handbook and looked at the policy regarding layoffs.

Tamara's company had a basic severance plan for anybody whose job was being eliminated: ten weeks of pay plus two weeks for every year of service. While there were no impending layoffs for her team, Tamara didn't think that when she left they would replace her with someone else at the same level. Her boss was cheap. Her department was always underfunded. She thought they might try to make the rest of the team absorb her job duties or hire a junior-level person to fill her shoes.

She took a risk and bet on herself. Instead of resigning, she scheduled a meeting with her boss and asked for and received a severance package. Tamara read the company's policies and crafted a script for herself that sounded a little something like this: "Hey, boss, I want to talk to you about my role. I've loved working for this company, but it feels like my time at this company is ending. When I was hired, the job duties required me to do a couple of specific things. My scope has changed, and I'm doing something different now. Do you understand how I feel?"

Then she went quiet and listened to her boss explain

that his hands were tied. He could talk to HR, but the company wasn't really in a position to change her job title or salary. Tamara remained poised and confident. She continued, "I hear you. The job I'm doing right now is not the job you hired me to do. I'm grateful for the opportunity, but I want to talk with you about another option: leaving with a plan. It might take me a week to find a job, but it might take me a year. I want to work with you and HR to find a win-win solution that includes leaving under the terms and conditions of our severance program. Would you join me for that meeting? I've already blocked some time on HR's calendar for later today."

Tamara read her boss's face—he seemed surprised, blindsided, and a little irritated. But he also couldn't wait to get her out of his office and run over to HR. The boss agreed to the meeting with human resources, and Tamara prepared for three options: be fired immediately (which was fine because she had another job lined up), be offered a different role with the company (which she would decline), or be given a severance payment. It took a day. Tamara was offered a severance plan. Her exit date was the following week, which was perfect timing for her new job. She left with eighteen weeks' worth of severance for a new job with a better title and more money.

Now, that's Tamara's story. And many HR professionals would prefer you didn't negotiate a severance payment on the way out the door. They would say it's risky and might get you escorted out of the building on the spot.

But if you have another job lined up and you want to take a chance, there are lessons for you in this story.

Put yourself first and ask.

One of my coaching clients found out her CEO was having an affair with his secretary, which is the worst cliché of all time. (Why can't CEOs have sex with somebody in procurement? Or maybe not have relationships with workers at all?) My client was upset and disgusted, so she went to her boss and said, "I'm done here because the CEO isn't living the values of the company. Let's make it easy for everybody by framing this exit as a redundancy. I'll sign whatever paperwork you need."

Severance pay worked well for both parties. The company was able to save face, and my client was able to move forward with her life while still paying her bills.

Another one of my clients worked for a company that was so toxic it was written about in three major American newspapers on the same day. My client couldn't stand to have her individual brand associated with the company's soiled reputation, so she conducted a super-secret job search and found a new role. She called me as she was about to hit send on the letter of resignation to the HR department, and I screamed, "NOOOOOOOOOOOOOOOOOO" into the phone.

Again, that's my great coaching style. My instincts are awesome.

You should never quit a job without asking for severance, *especially* when your company is in the news for corporate shenanigans. They will offer severance pay because they want you to feel good on the way out the door. Just kidding, it's because they don't want you to tell anybody where the bodies are buried.

Simply ask for the severance pay. Always. HR departments will cringe, but as with everything else, you never get what you don't ask for. Executives stuff a golden parachute into their employment agreements. Why shouldn't you?

Find an employment attorney to help you with language for your script, practice with friends, and prepare yourself for a few outcomes—you'll get paid, they will tell you no, or you'll be escorted out of the office for asking. But who cares if they fling you onto the sidewalk when you already have another job lined up? What matters is that you didn't leave money on the table and you continued to put yourself first.

EVERYBODY GOOD GETS FIRED ONCE

When I was in high school, I applied for a part-time job at a famous German restaurant in Chicago known for its sauerbraten and spaetzle. The manager told me he'd train me as a busboy for $3/hour plus a share of the tips. I accepted his offer on the spot, even though I'm not a boy.

My first night went by quickly as I shadowed other busboys, servers, and the hostess. I spent a few hours learning about the choreography of the restaurant floor. It was a chaotic dance, and I felt two steps behind. Toward the end of the evening, the manager noticed me milling around and asked me to collect the glass ketchup bottles and bring them to the back of the house. I'm a good kid. I do what I'm told. One by one, I went to each table and collected the ketchup bottles. To save time, I placed them all on a big serving tray. When I had all thirty-seven bottles lined up, I picked up the tray and began walking to the kitchen.

You know where this is going.

I took two steps, and the bottles fell to the floor. Glass shards went flying, and there was red, sticky ketchup everywhere—on my clothes, on the walls, and on the half dozen customers wrapping up their meals for the night. It looked like a German horror film. The manager rushed over and said, "Oh my God. In my thirty years in this industry, that is the stupidest thing I've ever seen anybody do. Get out of here. Don't come back."

Except I couldn't get out of there. I couldn't move. It felt as if my feet were stuck in ketchup and my heart had stopped. I might have blacked out for a moment, honestly. When I finally regained consciousness, I ran to the bathroom—sobbing and feeling humiliated. How could I be so dumb? Would anybody ever hire me again?

As I left the building, a server chased me down. He said, "Kid, that was the funniest thing I've ever seen in my entire life. You should have seen their faces—all of them. Thanks for a laugh. Here's your share of tonight's tips." He handed me a wad of cash. I got fired and still earned $200. In hindsight, not bad for a Friday night.

My friend Jennifer McClure is the host of the Impact Makers Podcast and a world-renowned keynote speaker and coach on leadership and branding. When people get fired, Jennifer has one piece of wisdom: everybody good gets fired once. You can't be a creative thinker or an innovator without pissing someone off. The greatest of the great will take that experience, learn from it, and improve the next time around. Failure and rejection are painful, but they are minor incidents in the bigger story of life.

I'm like, wait, hold the phone. Does everybody good get fired once? Is that true? Yes, okay, I was fired from a German restaurant. Does that count?

Jennifer told me we all have the potential to be great, even the sketchiest among us. Someone's dismissal *today* might be the wake-up call they need to turn it around *tomorrow*. And that's true. I've never worked in the restaurant industry again.

○ ○ ○

Meet a client of mine named Rachel. She was a director of cost accounting at a manufacturing company in Wisconsin. Cost accounting is the department that knows exactly how money is spent across an entire company, especially in a production environment. It can be a highly political job, but it's usually occupied by accountants who are not known for their emotional intelligence.

Rachel was different. She was bright and charming and had a passion for people. Yet she still got fired. Rachel initially liked her job, but she had one nemesis: the VP of logistics. His name was Eric, and this dude woke up every morning with the singular goal of causing trouble for the cost accounting department.

One day, Rachel got caught up in an email battle with Eric over something simple. (Isn't that how it always starts?) Rachel emailed Eric, and he responded with a slew of irrelevant questions that were a waste of time. She replied and copied the CEO and a few of his colleagues. He answered and copied even more people. The negativity escalated with each exchange. Rachel was passive-aggressive and acted like a victim. Eric was snarky and dismissive. With very little thought, Rachel ended an email message to Eric with fighting words: "You are a senior leader at this company, Eric. To say I'm disappointed with your behavior and communication skills is an understatement. Know better, do better."

You can't paraphrase poet and activist Maya Angelou in a racist and sexist system of work without consequences. With over fifteen people copied on the email message including the CEO, they fired Rachel within days for seeming insubordinate and not adhering to the value of "respectful communication" at the company.

Rachel found me on the Internet and wanted my help to locate her next job, figuring out exactly what went wrong in the last one. As we worked together, I learned that Rachel initially liked her job but saw warning signs from day one. Long before Eric was an asshole, there were signs that the culture didn't match the advertising on the career website. I asked Rachel what she learned about herself from this experience and what she'd do differently. She said, "No matter where I land, and for the rest of my career, I will always know a job is just a job. I'll give one hundred percent, but I'll keep my expectations low and make sure my priorities are aligned with my values." To Rachel, her priorities were simple: family, family, family. Those long hours at work trying to appease the CEO, Eric, and everybody else who thought they knew something about her department came at the expense of her relationship with her husband and children.

"There's a silver lining to getting fired," Rachel said. "My marriage was suffering because I was always on my computer and obsessing over work. I was unpleasant at home. I needed the universe to say, 'Focus on the important people who give you more than you're giving them.'"

Not everybody is as composed as Rachel after getting fired, though even she admitted it was tough on her ego for the first forty-eight hours. But after spending a day or two at home, she said, "I realized, my God, I missed all this time with my family because I was giving myself over to something that gives me a check every two weeks. I'm not proud of being fired, but I don't regret it."

We recently found Rachel a new job in cost accounting at another local company, and she's excited about forming healthy relationships with her leadership team, using the premortem to anticipate conflict, and prioritizing what matters most: her family.

○ ○ ○

People get fired every single day. Sometimes it is justified, sometimes it's bullshit, but it doesn't have to be devastating. There's never a good time to be fired, but it's always a good time to start putting your well-being first.

It starts with baby steps.

Step one: You are more than your job.

Step two: Even if you're not very good at your job, you're still a wonderful human being. Repeat that.

Step three: There are other jobs out there, and you'll find another one at some point.

Step four: Every day is a do-over, and, as long as you're breathing, you'll have time to try again.

Everybody good gets fired, once. I promise. Even you.

RESIGN WITH INTEGRITY

Sometimes, when I'm feeling bad about myself and need a pick-me-up, I think about all the people who have done stupid things at work. Once, an employee resigned and sent his boss a nasty email message. It was raw, vulgar, and angry. The boss found out where the employee would be working next and forwarded the message to the new HR department. The offer was rescinded, and the employee was now out of two jobs—his old one and his new one.

Another time, an employee went out for drinks on her last day of work. The entire team got hammered, and she admitted that she had negotiated a confidential severance payment. Word got back to our HR department, and the offer was rescinded to teach her—and future employees—a lesson about keeping your mouth shut.

But I've also watched honest, hardworking, ordinary people give their two weeks' notice and be escorted off the premises like criminals because someone in HR mistakenly thinks they'll be up to no good during those final two weeks. Giving your notice can be no big deal, or it can be a living hellscape.

When resigning, you have two goals—to communicate your last day of work and to wrap up any loose ends without making enemies. How do you do that without burning a bridge?

First, write a short letter or email that is clear and concise. I once had an administrative assistant resign via email. Her note seemed like she was requesting time off for therapy. I had to ask, Are you leaving or going out on medical leave? Because I couldn't tell. Learn from this lady and don't apologize or, worse, share the thirteen reasons you're saying goodbye. Just tell me you're done and state your preferred last day of work.

Don't plan your own going-away party. Nothing is more attention seeking and unprofessional than an individual who plans her own goodbye lunch or cocktail hour during work hours. If you do have a party and invite more than two people, invite everybody including your boss. And don't expect the company to pay for it, either.

Be available for an exit interview. When I say "be available," I mean show up with good intent and offer helpful feedback. They might not ask you for your opinion, but you should be prepared to offer constructive and positive feedback. Most of all, avoid being negative and petty. It's easy to start venting and throw your colleagues under the bus in an exit interview. My friend Julie Zhuo is a VP of product at Facebook and the author of *The Making of a Manager: What to Do When Everyone Looks to You.* She taught me to frame my feedback differently and ask, "What could have been done to make this experience twice as good?" The twice-as-good framework is helpful because it's positive and forward-looking, not judgy and condescending. Use this strategy to answer how your organization can make the work environment twice as good for future employees.

Quash gossip. Individuals with integrity don't gossip on the way out the door. If people wonder why you're leaving, answer candidly but dispassionately. You found another opportunity too good to pass up, or you wanted a role with bigger management responsibilities. Keep the story short and sweet, redirecting the gossip to something else. I'm confident there's something more scandalous happening in your office than your resignation. Let them find the drama elsewhere.

Refer candidates for jobs until the day you leave. The hardest thing to do in any company is hire someone good.

If you're really interested in maintaining a positive relationship with your company, refer good people for jobs—including yours.

It's possible to say goodbye to your former employer and hello to a new phase of your life without making enemies. Take what you've learned in this book. Be professionally detached, confident, and measured with your words. Think before you open your mouth. This isn't just good advice for giving your notice, it's wisdom that will help you put yourself first and take control of your career forever.

GOODBYES CAN BREAK YOUR HEART

People resign from work for all kinds of reasons. Maybe you landed your dream job out of the blue. Perhaps a recruiter approached you with an opportunity too good to pass up. Or maybe your spouse's job is forcing a relocation to another part of the world. Regardless, leaving a job can be bittersweet—for you and for your colleagues. If you love your boss or the people you work with, saying goodbye is often heartbreaking. Instead of rationalizing your emotions and pretending that nothing will change, it's important to honor your feelings and say what's on your mind. Don't leave without telling people how much they meant to you. Even if the words are inelegant and clunky, try.

My HR department once hired a twenty-two-year-old intern during the fall semester named Andy, and this poor kid became *the* talk of the town. With his shaggy blond hair and a tattered army jacket covered in patches, the desperate housewives of HR adored him. Including me.

I wasn't much older than Andy, but our lives couldn't have been more different. He passed the LSAT with flying colors and was preparing for the next phase of his life—backpacking through Europe before studying law. My life was a mess. My husband and I weren't married yet. We had broken up over my negative attitude about work and life. Instead of addressing my problems in therapy, I was stress-eating McDonald's McFlurrys and constantly complaining about my job.

Andy and I were in two separate universes, but we bonded over work. He was there with me in the early days of my career when I learned how to organize layoffs and memorized scripts to tell people that their livelihoods were ending. Together, we saw the devastation we caused and learned there's a better way to fire people—with empathy and compassion.

Andy was a great intern, but he also became a friend—and maybe more. He burned CDs with his favorite songs from the '90s for my travels, and he checked in on me when I was on the road. His collegiality was a sweeping departure from my relationship with the rest of our team, and it was nice to have a friend at work for the first time in a very long time. But relationships at work can be confusing, and most work friendships only exist in the bubble of work. People say they'll stay in touch forever. They rarely do.

Andy's internship was ending and he was moving on

to the next phase of his life, which made me sad. I thought about taking him out for dinner to celebrate his accomplishments during the past semester, but I didn't want my actions to be misconstrued. Well, actually, that's a lie. He was adorable. I wanted him to misconstrue my actions all night long, but my dumb HR job was getting in the way. I wasn't his direct boss, but I still felt like I had to live up to some invisible HR code of ethics. Why? Who knows? People, including me, overcomplicate life and relationships.

On his last day, the HR department ordered Andy a cake. If you know anything about HR, we'll order a cake for everything—birthdays, graduations, colonoscopies. We just love cake.

After we finished our dessert, and it was time to go home, Andy offered to walk me to my car.

We went out to the parking lot, and nobody was around. He handed me one final mix CD, and I knew it was goodbye. Suddenly, there were stars in my eyes and twinkly indie rock music in my ears. My heart rate spiked, and I began to sweat. I backed up to my driver's side door and opened my arms. Andy embraced me, and I hugged him with my twenty-pound laptop bag on one shoulder and my bulky purse on the other. It was a weird hug, but neither one of us wanted to let go. He looked down and went in for a kiss. I darted my head to the side and shook it.

"I can't," I blurted out. "I'm sorry."

Andy looked at me and said, "Come on. I feel like Pacey."

Then he turned around and walked away. I haven't seen him since.

Pacey Witter is a fictional character from a TV show called *Dawson's Creek*. I never watched it, but I learned that he was involved in a love triangle with characters named Joey and Dawson. In retrospect, maybe that's how Andy felt: in a convoluted love triangle with a girl and her job in HR. But I admire him for feeling his feelings and taking a shot—even though he was about to walk out the door. It takes a mature person to take a risk, put himself first, lean into feeling *human*.

If you have another opportunity lined up, leave and move forward. Say goodbye to your colleagues who helped you grow. Throw a party. Eat some cake. Reflect on how bittersweet it feels. Figure out if you're going to stay friends. And kiss the HR lady you've been hanging out with, even if she winds up awkwardly turning you down in the parking lot.

Take a risk. Just make sure you've submitted your letter of resignation first.

9

It's on You

TIPS TO FIX WORK IN SIX MONTHS

Be in love with your life, every detail of it.

—JACK KEROUAC

During the summer of 2019, nearly two hundred of the most respectable CEOs in America came together to change the future of work. They declared that corporations had a new mission: deliver value to customers, invest in employees, deal fairly and ethically with suppliers, and support the communities where their enterprise operates.

This declaration is called the "Statement on the Purpose of a Corporation."* It's a straightforward report that affirms a new vision: companies must adapt and

---

* https://opportunity.businessroundtable.org/wp-content/uploads/2019/12/BRT-Statement-on-the-Purpose-of-a-Corporation-with-Signatures.pdf.

change—becoming good stewards of people, communities, and the planet—if they want to survive and thrive.

Why did these CEOs feel the need to redefine the purpose of a corporation? Don't let me mislead you. This isn't a feel-good story about warmhearted leaders whose hearts have grown two sizes too big. These are realists who understood that the world of work has changed. They couldn't succeed in the twenty-first century with outdated, twentieth-century business models.

For the first time, five generations of workers are all uniformly sick and tired of broken, toxic environments. Work sucks, and people use social media platforms to talk about it. There are also more women and people of color in positions of power than ever before, and they are tired of waiting for change to happen. Tight labor markets have forced businesses to accept the notion that employees are both capitalists and *consumers of work*—people who can shop around for jobs, spending their time and energy anywhere.

In some ways, the declaration gives me hope. When the definition of a corporation changes, it alters the global discussion around work and provides room for a different conversation. For decades, there wasn't talk of raising the minimum wage, improving community relationships, reducing carbon footprints, or expanding charitable giving. There wasn't space for anything other than profits and losses. But now there is.

In other ways, a new declaration fixes nothing for people suffering at work right now. I'm talking about people like you, who struggle to wake up, wash your face, and spend another day in an organization that's incrementally eating your soul alive. And it wouldn't have helped me when I worked at Pfizer, either. It took a decade to recognize my own learned helplessness and get to Tijuana. Then it took another decade to establish and refine my success as a writer and public speaker. No CEO swooped in to help me out. It was on me to fix work. And it's still on you, too.

Fixing the global landscape of work is a formidable challenge. It requires corporations, government leaders, community organizations, consultants, and academics to examine centuries-old problems like racism, sexism, greed, and corruption.

But starting to fix your job demands a willingness to look at yourself in the mirror and ask, "What's on me?"

Don't wait for a group of CEOs to change your future. Change it yourself—and the sooner, the better.

PICK A NEW THING AND DO IT

When I worked at Pfizer, my life felt like the '90s movie *Groundhog Day*. Bill Murray plays a TV weatherman who experiences the same day repeatedly while visiting the town of Punxsutawney to report on an annual Groundhog Day celebration.

In a similar way, every day as an HR manager was the

same—crummy job, inane chitchat about the weather, pointless meetings, constant political battles, and tedious commutes home. But everything changed when I returned from Tijuana. I could no longer eat Starburst and drink Pepsi to manage my feelings. I had to adopt the habit of trying new things to refocus my attention and reframe my attitude, starting with one.

Why try one new thing? Well, many people forget that life isn't about their jobs. It's about relationships and experiences. Trying something new is an act of hope and a declaration of purpose. And I *really* needed a purpose beyond being somebody's local HR lady.

To get started with one new thing, I brainstormed a slew of activities I wanted to pursue but never had the time while working at Pfizer. Pilates. Cooking classes. Volunteering at the library. Going through my old clothes and donating everything that I hadn't worn in a year. Then, I wrote each activity on a piece of paper. I gathered all those ideas in a bag and plucked one out. I tackled that activity until I completed it or until I grew bored. Then I'd fish out another and start fresh.

As I introduced new activities into my daily habits, one by one, my frequent depressive patterns lifted. I grew less obsessed with work and more obsessed with feeling good. Life gradually became more satisfying. I took swimming lessons at the local athletic club. And once that was over, I enrolled in a creative writing class at the community college. Over the next few months, I also cleaned out my closets, went to the movie theater with friends, joined a book club, volunteered more, and gave extra attention to the dusty areas of my life that needed cleaning.

It might seem as if I was trying to distract myself by being busy. That's incorrect. My job didn't radically change. Only my worldview evolved. I remembered how much I loved being out in my community—realizing new things, meeting new people, laughing and having fun on a random Tuesday night.

Grab a notebook and envision six things you would do if you had the time. Then choose one. Get started today. Here are some ideas.

Take a cooking class. Read one chapter in a book every night before you go to bed. Explore your heritage on genealogy websites. Write thank-you letters. Volunteer at the local retirement community. Train for a 5K. Digitize your parents' old photos. Spend your evenings researching and planning your next vacation. Organize your bookshelves by color, subject, or even the Dewey decimal system. Bathe your dogs. Clean out your garage.

Accept accountability and spend your time and attention differently. My dream for you is simple: try something new. If you don't enjoy it, pick something else. You're choosing more than an activity or hobby—you're prioritizing yourself.

I'm betting on you and cannot wait to support you in that marvelous new endeavor.

GET A BEST FRIEND

One of my very best friends in the world is Lars Schmidt. He's not a German patriarch who drinks beer and walks around in lederhosen. He's just a regular guy who lives in Virginia (though who knows what he wears in the privacy of his home).

Years ago, Lars and I were strangers who attended a recruiting conference in California. He worked as a leader in the human resources department at National Public Radio. I owned a fledgling consulting business. Other than a few loose connections between us on LinkedIn, we did not know each other.

Recruiting conferences are notoriously dull, but Lars took the stage and expressed a passion for radically reinventing the world of work around talented employees. He asked people to stop thinking the worst of workers and start designing HR policies and programs that highlighted the best in employees. And he challenged the audience to be better versions of themselves, too.

In a teeming sea of Chico's clothing and Coach purses, I connected with a kindred spirit who shared a love of music, politics, and sticking it to the man. I was so blown away by his style and stage presence that I fought my way through the crowd and said, "I'm Laurie Ruettimann, and I want to work together."

There's nothing like having a best friend at work— someone who has your back on good days and bad.

Unfortunately, as a consultant and small business owner, I was a team of one and frankly felt a little lonely. And it doesn't matter the size or complexity of an organization. Loneliness is pervasive.

Cigna* is a worldwide health services organization based in Philadelphia, and it commissioned a study of loneliness and its impact on workforce productivity. The research would show that people who report weak relationships with their coworkers are 10 points lonelier than those who have strong ties. Isolated workers also think about quitting their job more than twice as often as non-lonely workers. And workers who reported being the loneliest were twice as likely to miss a day of work due to illness and five times more likely to miss work due to stress.

When I approached Lars, I wasn't deliberately trying to address my professional and personal loneliness. I thought I was inviting him to collaborate with me on nerdy HR projects like panel discussions and podcasts. But, in truth, I was subconsciously reaching out to him with a simple request: be my friend.

It would have been weird if I said, "Be my friend because the world is empty and I need someone to have my back. People are terrible, I need a safe place to vent, and I'd like to make someone's life brighter, too." Lars would have run the other way, and rightly so.

Instead, I offered a warm but clear invitation to

* https://www.cigna.com/about-us/newsroom/studies-and-reports/combatting
-loneliness/.

connect, which allowed him to say no. Thankfully, Lars took one look at me and said, "You bet, amiga. Let's get on a call."

Over the past ten years, my relationship with Lars has grown from trusted collaborator to brother-from-another-mother. He is an adviser, coach, mentor, and friend. I don't know what prompted me to recognize that I needed an honest-to-goodness friend in this world. But I'm so glad that I took a risk and asked Lars to connect.

Want to fix work for yourself? Look outside your immediate environment and seek individuals who share something in common with you. Maybe it's a passion for animals, or even a love of fancy cars. When you find someone, don't be afraid to take a risk and say, "We have something in common. I'd love to talk about it."

If they decline your invitation, keep looking. Don't think about all the people who turned you down. Rejection is just a moment in time. Think about the person out there who feels just like you—lonely, misunderstood, stuck—and who would enjoy having you in her life. Never stop searching for that significant, life-changing relationship.

Brené Brown has a saying: people, people, people. She's not wrong, but I would say: friends, friends, friends. The quickest path to happiness is to fix work by fixing it for a friend—even if that person isn't in your life just yet.

FIND YOUR PURPOSE IN
UNDER SIX MONTHS

I have a client named Leila who asked me to help her find purpose within six months. Why such a short, specific amount of time? She said, quoting the American cartoon character Popeye, "That's all I can stands, I can't stands no more."

Maybe you're too young to know anything about Popeye, but you're probably not too young to understand the sentiment. Leila's patience had long expired, her well-being was crumbling, and her attitude was super-negative. To cope with all the stress, she became addicted to Chick-Fil-A peppermint chocolate chip milkshakes.

"I've got six months to turn this around," Leila told me. "Or I will lose it."

As Leila's coach, I had questions: Why did she go to work? What were the core reasons she set her alarm and appeared at the office even though she'd rather be anywhere else? And how good are those milkshakes? I've never had one. (But I am very interested.)

I also needed to find out what she gained from work. Yes, it felt like torture. And yes, she was withering away on the inside. But the job paid her something—cash, health insurance, reasonably low expectations about her attendance. What was the currency that kept her coming back for more?

We had to define and explain the word *purpose*. After all, some people are spiritual while others are practical. I had to know if we were talking about a divine plan or a concrete road map to accomplish specific goals with her life.

If you're like Leila and struggling with work, I would like to ask you to join me in tackling difficulties to find your purpose within the next six months.

First, document the reasons you show up for work. You can use a sheet of paper, scribble in the margins of this book, or create an inventory in Microsoft To Do, Nozbe, or Google Slides. I'm ambivalent about where you write it. Just give me ten solid reasons why you go to work every day.

If you need some ideas, try these: Student loans. Rent. You can't find another job that pays more. You need new clothes. You send money to your family back home. You dream of retirement. You are saving for a new home. Your kid plays an expensive sport and you want to support her.

Don't overthink it. Sentence fragments are okay. If you struggle to get started, set a timer for five minutes. When it dings, walk away—even if you have written nothing—and try again tomorrow.

Once you have a list, you can move on to the next step.

Step two is telling me what you gain by going to work. Lay out the benefits you receive from your job. Here are some suggestions: Salary. Health insurance. 401(k) with or without company contributions. Paid time off. The satisfaction of providing for your family. A higher credit score. A possibility to shadow your boss during client visits and learn something new. Work travel to exciting cities. Access to new and emerging technology. Fun coworkers who always know when you're feeling blue. Meaningful work that fuels your soul.

If you're struggling to create a list of benefits, do the same thing as before and set a timer. Remember to walk away before you feel frustrated.

Done? You're ready for the final step, where we craft a clear statement on why you work and what you gain from the system.

> "I go to work to_____, and my job
> gives me _____."

Maybe you to go to work to pay rent, and your job gives you a paycheck. Or perhaps you go to work because you are saving for a down payment on a new home, and your job gives you financial security and stability. When I worked at Pfizer, my work-statement sentences looked like this:

"I go to work to pay off my student loans, and my job gives me a paycheck. I go to work to fund my future somewhere else, and my job gives me the autonomy and freedom to figure out my path. I go to work to earn enough money to donate to animal rescues, and my job matches my contributions 100 percent."

Even on the most oppressive days, this exercise helped me see I wasn't a victim. And neither was my client Leila, who went to work to pay her bills but had the autonomy to walk out of a bad meeting, drive to Chick-Fil-A, and get a milkshake when she was having a bad day. That's something.

As we continue to examine what is missing from your relationship with work, and with yourself, it's important to always return to the *why*. Because we each have a purpose. It just might not be what you're expecting.

o o o

My podcast producer, Danny Ozment, is a musician and singer. He was on his way to being an orchestra conductor when his daughter was born with cerebral palsy. It became necessary for Danny to work from home so he could manage his daughter's care—something incompatible with being a conductor. In a short amount of time, he had to overhaul his life. But where to start?

Danny returned to his roots as a musician and built a new life as a recording engineer working from home. Whenever he had a moment to himself—in the car, in the shower, settling down in the evening—he listened to podcasts.

Danny told me those podcasts brought him joy during times of great pain, and he realized his experience of recording and producing the human voice would benefit other podcasters and their listeners. But it wasn't enough for him to produce—there are a million offshore vendors who offer that service at a lower price. Danny visualized more. Successful podcasts thrive on community and a shared purpose. So he set out to be a teacher and coach who shares what he's learned about marketing and entrepreneurialism during his entrepreneurial journey.

Emerald City Productions is one of the premier podcasting companies in the world. He has a prestigious list of clients and provides immeasurable value to podcast hosts like me. He is also a sought-after keynote speaker and coach who advises on everything from digital marketing strategies to community building, working with leading business and creative professionals on almost all continents. And Danny has become a friend who reminds me that purpose is what you make of it.

Sometimes work is broken because our jobs suck and our paths are murky. Other times, our careers are upended for reasons beyond our control. But you can contribute and do great work without falling victim to the narrative that everything you do must have celestial, ethereal reasons. Sometimes providing for your family and being helpful is enough.

It's not uncommon to yearn for a purpose-driven life, but I suspect that the absence is more interesting than the purpose itself. Are you craving more meaning in your career? Do you miss something in your life that you can't describe? I'll tell you what I told my client Leila. Maybe you are making a bigger deal out of purpose than it deserves.

Purpose doesn't have to be the lofty or hyper-meaningful

reason you walk the face of the earth. It can just be a quiet conviction that motivates you to move forward when you face personal and professional challenges. Both options count.

Instead of striving to identify your purpose and demanding a more meaningful life in six months, determine what actions you would like to accomplish and craft a plan.

Try filling in the blanks of this sentence:

"In the next six months, I would like to _____. So I need to _____."

When I asked Leila to fill in the blanks, she wrote, "In the next six months, I would like to take a vacation and turn off my phone. So I need to plan a trip and work with my associates so I can have a much-needed break."

Okay, not a bad start.

She also wrote, "In the next six months, I would like to be happier. So I need to call my employee assistance program and explore what's missing in my life."

That's better. *Much* better. What are your sentences?

o o o

Change is slow and incremental, but it happens. This book offered a bevy of tools and tips to put yourself first, prioritize your well-being, and be your own HR department. We covered how to fight back and reclaim your work–life balance, work smarter instead of harder, bet on yourself, learn something new, fix your money, be your own advocate at the office, look for new work opportunities, and leave with dignity.

But nothing changes if you don't take that initial risk, bet on yourself, and put yourself first. You can't continue to blame other people if work is broken. Fix it for yourself.

I know that many of the recommendations in this book are daunting. But what I recommend for you, I've done myself. Fifteen years ago, I was a girl who worked in HR and couldn't run a mile. Five years ago, I was a writer and a consultant who ran marathons but still hadn't written a book. Five months ago, I still didn't know if this book would see the light of day. Five days ago, my younger brother called me and said that he was diagnosed with stage III colon cancer.

What's my purpose now? I want to be the best sister possible. Everything else pales in comparison. And, yet, I still have a job to do.

No journey is easy, no path to success is straightforward, and no life exists without heartache and pain. But your job shouldn't impede your quality of life, either. So, if you hate work and complain about how it's broken, ask yourself, *What have I done today to put myself first and finally take control of my career?*

Answer those questions and that's how you fix work once and for all.

Further Resources

Betting on You, the book, is over.

But betting on yourself is only just beginning.

Please visit bettingonyoubook.com for conversation starters, checklists, and action plans to put yourself first and finally take control of your career.

Then head over to laurieruettimann.com/speaking to learn more about how Laurie delivers highly personalized and entertaining lessons on work, life, and leadership to audiences worldwide.

Acknowledgments

Writing a book proves that it's a wonderful life.

Before there were words, there was a dream. Thanks to Nick Morgan and Sarah Morgan at Public Words for helping me think long thoughts in short sentences. And thanks to Esmond Harmsworth for being my agent and mentor (and the person who took me to my first Broadway show!), and Libby Burton for changing my life.

The team at Henry Holt have been dream partners. Special thanks to my talented editor Ruby Rose Lee for believing in this book and working hard to bring the manuscript to life. Additional thanks to Serena Jones, Maggie Richards, Amy Einhorn, Patricia Eisenmann, Caitlin O'Shaughnessy, Grazia Rutherford-Swan, Jason Liebman, Marian Brown, Sarah Crichton, and Chris O'Connell for collaborating to deliver the best version of this book to market.

I'm grateful for the input and candid advice from Vadim Liberman, Jennifer McClure, Lance Haun, Lars Schmidt, Tim Sackett, William Tincup, Carmen Hudson, Mary Faulkner, Steve Browne, Kathleen Brenk, Carla Schull, Steven Sims Maginel, Carlos Escobar, Susana Stoll, April Matan, Rana Fahey, Jason Todd, and Sarah Brennan. Thanks for having my back online and IRL.

No woman is a failure with friends. I'd also like to recognize Mary Ellen Slayter, Sam Weston, Don MacPherson, Devon McGrath, and Fred Leong who spotted me on the streets of New York City right after my first meeting with the team at Henry Holt. Thanks for helping me overcome my doubts over the past ten years and see the value of being "HR famous."

I have a magnificent crew that offers love and support in North Carolina. I want to acknowledge Kathy Howard, Kristi Martinson, David Fruchter, Heather Cruz, Magy Isidro Tome, and Martha Lopez for having my back, taking care of the cats, and helping me run my business. Additionally, I'd like to recognize the experts who treated me with compassion and kindness along the way: Dr. Don Troyer, Dr. Linda Harpole, Dr. Paul Andrews, Dr. Daniel Guerron, and Dr. Peregrine Kavros.

I want to thank my parents, siblings, and in-laws for their quiet but unmistakable support. Each person's life touches so many others. They've influenced mine, and I'm grateful for it.

Finally, I'd like to acknowledge Ken Ruettimann for

walking into my office and asking me to lunch. Everybody should have the opportunity to be loved the way this man loves me. What should we do next, Kenny? What do you want? You want the moon? Just say the word, and I'll throw a lasso around it and pull it down. Hey. That's a pretty good idea. I'll give you the moon.

But first, let's rescue a dog.

INDEX

ABOUT THE AUTHOR

Kathy Howard

Laurie Ruettimann is a former human resources leader turned writer, entrepreneur, and speaker. CNN recognized her as one of the top five career advisers in the United States, and her work has been featured on NPR and in the *New Yorker*, *USA Today*, the *Wall Street Journal*, and *Vox*. She frequently delivers keynote speeches at business and management events around the world and hosts the popular podcast *Punk Rock HR*. She lives with her husband and cats in Raleigh, North Carolina.